not black

inside words from the
Bronx WritersCorps

edited
by
Mary Hebert

Plain View Press
P.O. 33311
Austin, TX 78764
512-441-2452
sbpvp@eden.com

The Bronx Council on the Arts WritersCorps Project is made possible in part by
the National Endowment for the Arts with Funds from AmeriCorps and adminis-
tered by the Associated Writing Programs. Additional funding is provided by the
Joe and Emily Lowe Foundation, Wendling Foundation, Greentree Foundation,
Booth Ferris Foundation, H.W. Wilson Foundation, American Express Founda-
tion, New York Times Foundation, Chemical Bank, Citibank, Con Edison, EMK
Enterprises, Reed Foundation, New York State Department of Education, New
York State Council on the Arts/New York City Department of Cultural Affairs-
Cultural Challenge Program, the Office of the Bronx Borough President,
Fernando Ferrer, The Bronx Delegation to the City Council and individual
contributors.

Cover Art:
Soho Summer by Juan Goméz Quiróz
58" x 58" acrylic on canvas.
Cover Art Photo © 1995
by: D. James Dee

This book was made possible by funding from the WritersCorps and the Reed
Foundation.

This material is based upon work supported by the Corporation for National
and Community Service under AmeriCorps Grant No. 94ADSDC029. Opinions or
points of view expressed in this document are those of the authors and do not
necessarily reflect the official position of the Corporation for National Service or
the AmeriCorps program.

Acknowledgments

Thanks to Chris Belden and Steven Sapp for their help in shaping this book at its beginning stages, and in conducting and transcribing the writer's interviews; to Chris Belden and Ronaldo Wilson for their excellent proof-reading of the manuscript and again to Chris for his advice throughout the editorial process; to Wayne Providence for photo portraits, Juan Gómez Quiróz for cover art, to Sandra María Esteves for art work, to Bill Aguado and Geri Hayes for their support and belief in this anthology; to Paulette Beckford, Laurie Palmieri, and Keith Roach for their helpful assistance; to Margo LaGattuta for the introduction to Plain View Press; to publisher, Susan Bright, for her vision; and to Jane Alexander and the staff at the National Endowment of the Arts for their enthusiastic support and efforts on behalf of this project.

Individual works have been published in the following publications: Isamu Noguchi quoted in "The Way of the Earth," *"Encounters with Nature in Ancient and Contemporary Thought,"* by T.C. McLuhan, A Touchstone Book, published by Simon & Shuster, © 1994 by T.C. McLuhan, p.157. Excerpts from jennifer jazz's *"bronx brazil,"* printed with permission from jennifer jazz, © 1995 by jennifer jazz. *"Closing the 20th Century"* was first published in *"Concertos on Market Street,"* Kemetic Images Press, 1993, © Jesús Papoleto Meléndez. *"Encouraging Nurturing Behavior of Two- to Seven-Year-Olds by Introducing Plants and Flowers,"* by Karen Green, reprinted with permission from Haworth Press, Inc., © 1994 by the Haworth Press, Inc. All rights reserved.

The Bronx Council on the Arts would like to thank the following participating schools and community organizations whose commitment to community helped make the first year of WritersCorps, and this anthology, possible.

Aging in America
Maria Uzovich, Director, CTR
Betances 146 Community Center
James Beale, Director
Betances 401 Community Center
Carrie Jones, Director
Bronx Lebanon Hospital
Betty Cole
Director of Volunteer Services
Bronx Satellite Academy
Kelson Maynard
Tony Schwab
Judith Scott
Bronx Museum of the Arts
Jerri Allyn
Jane Delgado, Executive Director

Citizens Advice Bureau
Rebecca Ayala
Carolyn McLaughlin, Executive Director
Vivian Vasquez
Community Elementary School 235
Felix Gonzalez, Principal
Lucia Hernaiz, Bilingual Teacher
Terry Hirsh, Teacher
Marty Markoe, Computer Teacher
Tom Nieves, Staff Developer
Carlos Nunez, Art Teacher
Mona Padilla, Librarian
Lucy Rivera, Administrative Assistant
Housing Enterprise for the Less Privileged (H.E.L.P.)
Susan Cahill, Executive Director
Ronald Lovelle

Hostos Center for the Performing Arts, Hostos Community College
Wally Edgecombe, Director, Center for Arts and Culture
Jackson Community Center
Ronald Parker, Director
Junior High School 149
Muriel Eingert
Junior High School 183
Jaqueline Killip, Assistant Principal
Milton Polsky, Development Teacher
Latin American Writers Institute
Isaac Goldemberg
Middle School 135
Jocelyn Rodriguez, Teacher
Mind Builders Creative Arts Center
Camille Akeju, Executive Director
Lorraine McFarland
Moore Community Center
Trini Jones, Director
Morrisania Air Rights Community Center
Shirley Marshall, Director
Mosaic Beacon Center
Betty Aderman, ESL Instructor
Karen Brown, Resource Development
Bill Yakowitz, Director
Mosholu Preservation Corp.
Jordan Moss
Dart Westphal
Mt. Carmel Center for Senior Citizens
Michelle Imperiale, Director
North Bronx-Westchester Neighborhood Restoration Association (NBWNRA)
Dorothy DeLayo, Executive Director
Lisa Ibarra
New York Botanical Gardens
Glenn Phillips
New York City Housing Authority, Bronx South District
Gary Morgan, District Supervisor
Monray Whiteside, Asst. District Supervisor

Pelham Parkway North Lunch Program
Roberta I. Cohen, Director
Pepatian
Pepon Osorio
Merian Soto
Phipps Community Development Corp.
Manuel Mendez
The Point Community Development Corp.
Paul Lipson
Mildred Ruiz
Maria Torres
PS122-Marble Hill School
Doris Budow, Alternative Assessment Coordinator
Dr. Sheldon Lindenbaum, Principal
South Bronx Community Action Theatre
Fred Daris, Executive Director
Tilden Towers II Senior Center
Harold Payne, Director
Wave Hill
Madeline Keeve
West Farms Beacon School
Eddie Calderone-Melendez

We are a landscape
of all we have seen.

Isamu Noguchi

Table of Contents

2   *alone*   130

Not Black and White—
Introductory Notes

by Mary Hebert, Editor

"Not Black and White" is a work of the heart. It is because we have a president who listened to his heart-wisdom that WritersCorps exists; it is the heart-wisdom of the participating writers that led us to this program in the Bronx; it is the heart of the Bronx that we tried to connect with and evoke.

We, the writers, conceived this anthology to provide a forum for our heartfelt experience—our joys and frustrations—as co-creators of the first Bronx WritersCorps. The writer interviews, conducted by myself, Chris Belden and Steven Sapp, explore our choices as writers, and our visions of the role writing can play in community and culture. The interviews are followed by samples of each writer's participant work, and finally, the writer's own work.

Among the voices of our participants are many whom not only have never written before, but never imagined they had anything to say. Our role in WritersCorps was not that of teachers, delineating the rules of writing; we were facilitators who tried to create a safe place for these "young" voices to emerge amid the rattle-screech of urban life that threatens to drown us all. Thus in putting our participant writing to the page, we felt it was crucial to the spirit of this project to leave their work intact, as much as possible. While this results in some inconsistencies throughout the text, it also allows the reader to experience first hand, as we did, the vitality of these unique voices.

These stories and tellings and poems are written in the heart's language—the language of blood and air and gravity. This language is not black and white, but like our blood is all variations of blue and red. Despite constant pressure from all our "big brothers" in mass media and big business to polarize society and diminish the complex needs of human survival to issues of race, gender, age and class, the truth persists, and is evident in these voices: we are not simply black and white, old and young, homeless and housed, we are the truth underneath that is all the colors of the human spirit.

by Geri Hayes,
Director of Public Programs
Bronx Council on the Arts

This book offers a glimpse at magic that took place in the Bronx in 1994 and 1995. Though it often passes unnoticed by outsiders, there is a great deal of magic happening here all the time. Those of us who live and work here notice; it feeds our soul, recognizing and celebrating our humanity, embracing our scars along with our beauty. This magic is our art: the music, dance and poetry that emerges from our splendid diversity.

The Bronx WritersCorps Project placed literary artists in over twenty-five sites in the Bronx to create literary venues that would build community by creating links between individuals and organizations. The artists' presence at these sites strengthened the organizations' effectiveness and helped each promote its mission in a concrete way: by facilitating individual creative expression through writing. Out of these unique partnerships came the voices of the participants recorded in this book: seniors sharing their journey, homeless women articulating their pain, adolescents describing the world through their eyes, elementary school students revealing their maturity and innocence.

The vital groundwork of the Bronx Council on the Arts, and the vision of its Executive Director, Bill Aguado made this program a success. In fulfilling its commitment to serve the needs of the community, the Bronx Council has worked instinctively and strategically in recent years toward integrating art into the essence of community. That goal demanded that the Council transform itself, change from being a provider of information and resources into an interpreter of community needs—a simple concept with a complex design.

WritersCorps enabled the Bronx Council on the Arts to extend this vision in a dramatic and concrete way. By creating multiple points of entry into the Bronx community, it brought this eclectic group of gifted writers to sites where our children come to learn, our seniors come to talk, and our community residents come to enrich their lives. *"Not Black and White "* records this integration of writers and community; it is a telling of the tales and songs heard there—the tales and songs of our community.

by Bill Aguado, Executive Director, Bronx Council on the Arts

The anthology you are about to experience is a culmination of skill, talent and dedication by the members of the Bronx WritersCorps—eighteen writers who are as different in experience and age as the populations they served. Yet, they all shared a commitment to community service and the power of the written word, a power that has provided enormous strength and dignity to the people of The Bronx. This commitment to public service is consistent with AmeriCorps, a subsidiary of the Corporation for National and Community Service—the brainchild of President Clinton.

Initiatives like WritersCorps do not happen by accident. It was the vision of Jane Alexander, Chairman of the National Endowment for the Arts, who first conceived of this vital program. Like all important visions it needed professionals to shape it into a workable program, and to them: Diane Matarazza, Director of the Locals Program and Gigi Bradford, Director of the Literature Program, both of the NEA, I extend my thanks. The burden of implementing and administering the National WritersCorps program—no small task to say the least—was left in the capable hands of Mark Johnson and Diem Jones of the Associated Writing Programs.

A special thanks to the funding sources in New York City that supported the outreach efforts of WritersCorps—the Joe and Emily Lowe

Foundation, the Greentree Foundation, the Booth Ferris Foundation, the New York State Council on the Arts, the New York City Department of Cultural Affairs Cultural Challenge Initiative and individual contributors. Yet this anthology would not have been possible without the encouragement and financial support of Jane Gregory Rubin and the Reed Foundation.

To the staff of the Bronx Council on the Arts—Geri Hayes, Laurie Palmieri, Melanie Smith and Toni Roberts—thank you for your dedication in helping WritersCorps become the prototype of community service that it is, and to my Board of Directors, who remain steadfast in their commitment to the arts and The Bronx, a debt of gratitude payable by this anthology.

Lastly, and perhaps most importantly, to the members of WritersCorps who remained committed to the spirit of AmeriCorps and the communities served, we are forever in your debt.

by Jane Alexander, Chairman
National Endowment for the Arts

When President Clinton signed the legislation that created AmeriCorps in 1993, he envisioned a national force of citizens dedicated to making a difference in America's towns and cities. The President sought to tap the spirit, energy and idealism of our young people to help renew America—community by community, block by block, person by person. These "inside words" from the Bronx Council on the Arts are an eloquent reflection of the success that WritersCorps projects have accomplished elsewhere under the direction of the San Francisco Art Commission and the Washington, DC Commission on the Arts and Humanities, in partnership with the Corporation for National Service.

AmeriCorps*WritersCorps is a national collaboration that uses the power of the written word to increase literacy levels and to strengthen skills and capacities needed for productive citizenship. In the process, by providing an avenue for creative expression, it offers an alternative to violence, substance abuse and despair. Administered by the National Endowment for the Arts, it places writers in underserved and challenged neighborhoods to work with residents in unlocking imagination through language. Participants range in age from seven to one-hundred-and-three; and in cultural, ethnic, and racial background they mirror America in all its splendid diversity. Social service, community activists and local schools provide assistance and venues, making the program a genuine community effort. The National Endowment for the Arts is proud of this important venture involving creativity and community. Reading this fine anthology, one is sure to see why.

Dreaming

I am dreaming.
In my heart
are three rivers
that flow through
these Bronx streets
death
sex

& smiling children.

Keema W.
H.E.L.P. Bronx

1.

Steven Sapp
Chris Belden
Ronaldo V. Wilson
Willard Cook
Jennifer Webster
William H. Banks, Jr.
Paolo Corso
Don Gellver
jennifer jazz

S teven Sapp is an actor, choreographer and playwright. A graduate of Bard College, he has written, directed and choreographed 6 theatrical productions, including *"Purgatory"* and *"Another I Dies Slowly."* He is cofounder of The Point Community Development Corporation and creator of *"Live From the Edge"* theatre project. As a member of the Bronx WritersCorps, he worked with underserved youth in the Hunts Point section of the Bronx.

I'm a writer because it's the best way—the only way—for me to deal with my feelings, and with my surroundings as they change. I didn't like talking when I was a kid, but when it came to writing I felt extremely confident. When you see that you can have an effect on people, you say, "Wow. I evoked that feeling. Maybe I can do it again."

In elementary school, I was in the advanced class, and my teacher—his name was Gary Simon—gave us novels to read. We were reading books in the 2nd and 3rd grade. My mother bought tons of books, so instead of watching television I would pick up a book; I also read a lot of comic books. My imagination was stimulated, and I went from reading to writing my own stories.

Writers invoke thought, and stimulate—hopefully—some confidence within, which in turn, helps you deal with the ills of society. I feel very strongly that writing helped me develop confidence and perspective. A lot of people who I grew up with lost confidence when it came to life in general, with being responsible. I was writing and dealing with my stuff at least on paper—I wasn't internalizing everything. That, in turn, put me in a situation where I had options, and because of my creativity, I was better able to look at those options and make choices. A lot of my friends internalized everything and saw no options at all.

What I try to teach my students is not necessarily to be a writer, but to be a person who thinks. If you think about what's going on with you constantly, and deal with it, then you can start looking for options and figure out how to deal with the next level.

Plays, poetry—all the creative forms—just reflect society back and make it interesting to look at. A piece can be about something that's really out—it can take you on a trip. What I try to do in my work, especially my plays, is to take people on a trip, and make them deal with things in a completely different way. Like eating cereal with a spoon all your life, and then one day you eat it with a fork—it's a completely different perspective.

Writers give people different angles on life. You may read something on a topic you thought you knew, and it blows you away. Somebody close to you may have died, and you read something that comforts you at that moment, or elevates you to a different plane. All the creative arts are very spiritual, I believe. It keeps you human, in a sense, while—in the real world—we're getting into realms that are not human. The arts can keep you grounded.

16

WritersCorps for me is very personal because I grew up in the Bronx. I was around social programs—if you grow up in the inner city, there are always social programs. For me, to be able to grow up here, go to college, then come back here as an artist—a teacher—is very rewarding. I always wanted to do it, but I didn't know how. So it's very good to be back in the old neighborhood, doing what I'm supposed to do, which is teach. So WritersCorps was just another step along the path. It's not something I had to think twice about doing.

My experience with WritersCorps has been enlightening in ways other than I expected. I knew it would be a lot of work, but it's been rewarding indirectly. It's also pushed me to take my work more seriously. Being around the other writers—seeing their work habits— has also pushed me, made me think. I'm more intrigued than some, also, in the administrative aspects of art. I think you should be able to understand and control the product as well as create it. The political stuff in the program doesn't sidetrack me at all.

The mission of WritersCorps, at this stage, is to be consistent. You're not going to see results after one year. Being here consistently as a program will bring the community together, and show—yes, this is a real program, we're here for the long haul; this is a serious effort to teach and provide literacy to the neighborhoods. Hopefully, I'll be able to provide a spark in somebody, and as I'm developing my own work, they're developing also. Because I bring my students in on my own creative process, they can see what goes on—that it's not some magical Walt Disney thing. They'll see that they are writers also. Then they can take it to the next level.

17

Steven Sapp

Games People Play

by Freddie Brown

Bang Bang, you're it.
Bang Bang, you're it,
no tag back, motherfucker.
Blang, Blang, Blang.
Innocent church, boy down
as he frowns at the games
we play in his playground.
Rich nigga,
poor nigga,
when will you learn we are
free...

Mr. Rogers lay back
while June Bug sells his crack
in our neighborhood
but the only faces
incarcerated are black.
So why did we sing the blues?
Cause we'll always pay dues
in blood sweat and tears
as long as there's
hundred dollar shoes.

So Mister Rogers, can I sell
in your neighborhood
near your rivers and plains
and service your people
with your poison for veins?
And bring our wargames
into your backyard
and if one of
your lives are lost, ask you not
to take it so hard or what's up
with your son, can he hang
with my crew and play cops
and robbers like you force us to?

But of course your reality's
a one-sided coin.
We are taught to unite
but somehow never joined.
My people kill my kind and others
kill their kind while you stay
in exile using media to remind us
of our faults and oppressive
type ways while we bury each
other and pay you for our graves.

Arizona Prayers
by Chris Hayes

Quick foot winds
hurl my body against
the hot red clay
shattering into

a million firm
terra cotta
fragments

ground from
dirt and blood,
flavored

with ancient prayers
sung
by young widows.

My body rises,
drafts of Arizona winds
blow hot
like coyotes chased
wildly
by ancient deities—

the quiet woodless
forest,
inhabited by ancient spirits
above medieval fire,

haunted by the voices
of the elders
bouncing
along the slope
of the
mesa.

I stand at the
pinnacle
of creation,
within the cavernous enclosements
of the Creator
whispering powerfully

to invisible
demons

and long neglected angels.

Steven Sapp

Heart's Reflection

by Dominick Lee

A Kiss
An Image that reflects
Velvet light
Off the smoothness
Of her lips

Her touch
A gateway to long forgotten
Sensations
Desires only granted to lesbians
And kings

Her skin
Brown diamond
A tribute to the gods of
Amber and fire

The covenant of her love
Fantasy recreated
In emerald light
Sensuality encased in
A smell of jasmine
And a touch of poison

I move through these
Memories
Entranced, enveloped
Then shattered by the sheer
inequity
of unresolved passion

But, then rapture turns into reality
Unrelenting truth into pain
Then tears

Her death, has left me
A clairvoyance of sorts
The curse to look beyond the grave

And fall in love
With an intimate ghost
Who's soul I cannot possess
And whose haunted specter
Shall hold me in its embrace
For eternity

Fifteen

by Steven Sapp

She is fifteen
just a baby some say
don't know which way is up
but knows she wants to be down.
Her virginity
M.I.A.
she would say
stolen by her mother's pet dog
or was it a snake
who comes to pluck the apple night after night
but does not take a bite
it just
burrows his way inside, where he thinks it is soft
and warm.
His presence huffs and puffs and blows down
her walls,
a torn...ado, turning her white slippers ruby red,
destroying all it sees,
like the twister that picked up Auntie Em's house
and turned Dorothy around and around in the air.
He promised to take her over the rainbow
but when the twister was over
there was no land of Oz
only somebody who called himself a Wizard.
His throne room was only her room.
When she looks behind the curtain
all she sees is her mother's boy toy.
I guess there's no place like home.
There's no place like home.

Her mother does not listen to this hit record
as it plays—
"You probably heard it somewhere else.
It's all been said and done before
and much better, so let it go!"
And she tries
but the record keeps skipping and skipping

and skipping and skipping and skipping
and skipping and skipping and skipping
and skipping and skipping
past
what was once pure into something
that has been stepped on
cut with something
diluted
watered down into something you ingest
will take your ass on a trip
but won't go straight to your brain or to your heart.
This trip comes to her at night.

She calls it a dream because anything can happen—
in a dream
herself she reminds, until she believes
she has to believe
in—
a fairy godmother—
who will explain the unexplainable
and show her how to click
those ruby red slippers together
and find her true home
called— Someday.

Steven Sapp

Ramblings of a Funky Junkie

Words unrehearsed spill
and I wake to hear them
I feel every four-letter treat, spoken with love and bite
and
whatever other daily delights flow
from the lips of the living dead
sitting in the traditional Black and Blue lighting
of my ancestors
I groove to the lingo of the urban bass—
that deep bass.
When I dance in that rhythm
I am home.
(sings) Do you love me, Do you love me
now that I can dance. *(stops)*

Ghetto hands reach to me and call me son
more than you ever did, *Daddy*
or *Popi*
or whatever you call yourself now.
The street had to show me how to dance
and you ladies know how much
you love a guy
who knows how to dance.
Shit!
Even an ugly guy can get a woman
if he got the steps
how to get in and make the music
follow you . . . almost
to make the other dancers watch you
and dream
but there was one dance that I love to do.
Some call it the nod
but I call it the feelgood.

(sings)
First you grab your arm and you pull up your sleeve.
Look for the vein, you better hit it right Steve.
Slap on the arm, pump up the vein.
I could almost feel it now going straight to the brain.
Take the needle, shoot your shit, no AIDS please.
Fuck around and catch that government disease.
Can you feel it baby, are you ready for the ride.
This shit is better than suicide.
I'm the man, I'm the man.
Do you love me? Do you love me?
Now that I can dance.

I.R.T. Number 6

by Steven Sapp

Late night, I.R.T. No. 6
to the Bronx
Got my ghetto stroll down to a synchronized perfection
my expression understanding its usual mission
does not betray me this night.
It is ready in its locked and load position
suggesting readiness to explode if necessary.
I carry my physical in the same vein
a catlike pulse
putting my eight lives on the line
it should be nine but I lost one
when I fell in love the first time
the virgin voyage that promises forever
but steals a piece of your soul named innocence.
Who gives a damn about this inner sense
reserved for the mental of children?
Adulthood convinces us that it's expendable
so I ride this horse or Pandora's Box
with the other weeds who have found a way
through the cracks.
I listen to some young brothers, *Signifying*—
They speak in tongues while their vocal chords
hang from trees, microphones and basketball rims.
They got that verbal herbal down pat
bending their bodies to fit the words.
They see me, watching.
I see them, watching.
We both understand and give a silent nod.

   Respect.
Enter into the mix, a group of similac girls
or is it steroids
"It's gotta be something they putting in the food,"
screams an old man sitting across from me.
I smile, another nod.
The brothers circle like they've been taught to do
lessons learned from rolling stone papas
these dark gables, they think they control this game

25

and the sweet young things like the competition
squeezing their thicknessessssss and youthfulnesssssss
into one big United Mistake of America
they will take the road most traveled
hoping some man can be their personal Moses
    deliver them from their bondage
      and part their red sea.

I watch this ritual from the outside
        as usual
I never learned how to play the game this way.
I played by my own rules—
a quiet instrumental of unrehearsed music
while she and me conduct
in the greatest concert of them all.
Damn somebody stinks in here.
It crashes through the montage of rhythms
that accompanies my ride.
I don't acknowledge it.
It's only the thunder before the lightning—
"Pleeeeze/ can somebody help me/
You see I'm kinda having a bad life/
So I think/ I mean I know/ I mean I wish/
I mean I hope/You gotta little love/
in your heart tonight cause I am/
the hardest working man in this business.
But I've watched my tears
stolen from me, bottled and sold as perfume
aftershave lotion, called revolution—
So could you/ would you, can you/
    Pleeeeze, give a brother some change?"

Nothing is said, eyes become picture perfect
      Still
my eyes challenge the voice
I reach for spare jingle in my pocket.
crusty hand reaches for mine
a quick transaction I hope.
I'll give some money but not much more.

26

Eyes lock.
I know this man.
Larry from back in the days
PS 140, Mr. Simon's gifted class.
I know this man.
Words hide from me, as they do him.
I remember Larry teaching me how to do the handshake
like the big boys.
I never forgot
neither does he
as he gives me shake and completes the transaction.
He continues on his quest for the jingle.
My eyes wait for his again.
He never turns.
As he leaves, he says
"God bless and
thank you for letting me be myself again."
With that he is gone, leaving me with seven lives now.
And I never spoke.
Damn.

Chris Belden was born and raised in Canton, Ohio, attended the University of Michigan, and currently lives and writes in New York City. He is co-author of the feature film, "*Amnesia,*" due out in 1996. As a WritersCorps member, he worked at several senior citizen centers, conducting oral history interviews and creative expression workshops.

I'm a writer for purely selfish reasons. Writing allows me to have a voice, and at the same time it brings order to what I perceive as a chaotic world. When I was growing up, it was emotionally chaotic for me. People were unpredictable. I was not encouraged to speak up, and found a lot of solace in reading. You can read a story in which all kinds of horrible things—murder and chaos—happen, but it's still only a story. When you're writing, it's even better because, as the author you're in complete control, as with most art.

When you're done reading a book, it's like getting a little taste of immortality. I always remember when I finished *"David Copperfield,"* I wept like a baby. I wept because it was this big fat book with this amazing character, going through these amazing adventures, told in the most mesmerizing way. When it was over, I was horribly sad that the story had ended, yet I was still alive. It's the same with any book that's extraordinarily connected to your emotions—and you'll only read a few like that in your lifetime. Even stories that don't touch you quite that way, they still touch something. You hope, anyway.

I was very influenced by films as a kid. I loved horror movies. Horror movies let loose the chaos in a sense. I studied film in college; I've made films. I'm very visually oriented, and when I write fiction I'm always thinking of what it looks like.

I came to WritersCorps having gone through many years of writing workshops as a student. I felt I had a good foundation for what it would take to run a workshop. Basically what I had learned was the difference between the writer and the narrator, how to establish a mood and a tone, and being conscious of the decisions you make as a writer. Some of these ideas are awfully lofty and, frankly, of no interest to people who are 102 years-old and just wanting to get their stories out before they pass away. At the same time, some people will get it, and those who don't get it entirely may come away with something.

If I have a future as a teacher, I'd like to be with students who don't consider themselves the great American novelists, who just want to write some stories and have fun. My WritersCorps students are not out to make a million bucks. They're out to see what they can do, to share stories with their children and grandchildren, to relive certain things, and stretch their imaginations. With some of them I've been very successful.

There's no way we can say where WritersCorps will go from here, but I think most of us have touched people on an individual level. When you get down to it, writing is about one person alone with a pen, a piece of paper and their imaginations. Whether I'm working with five people or fifteen, it's still about that person alone at home, trying to write a page or two. When they do that—that's when WritersCorps is working.

With any luck WritersCorps will continue and this group of senior citizens will begin to develop a sense of power in being able to express themselves. I see people who are happier with themselves, doing things they never thought they could, at an age when they didn't think they could do something new. They have a new reason to leave the apartment—a new purpose.

The other way WritersCorps can make a difference is to literally bring people in the community together. In my case, a small group of senior citizens and a small group of 7th graders, over a period of time, developed a relationship of sharing and respect and found a common ground. One senior in my workshop is now a pen pal with one of the kids. They did this on their own.

That's a drop in the bucket. It's not going to mean anything to Jesse Helms. But if WritersCorps keeps going, it will mean something to a whole lot of people in one neighborhood in the Bronx. And if WritersCorps were in every town and city, it would mean something in all those places.

Growing Up on a Farm, Part I

by Cora Green
Tilden Towers II Senior Center

My grandfather owned his farm and had a big house, so my mother and father lived there, plus two uncles and an aunt and her husband. Everyone called my grandmother, "Mama," including me, and I really thought that she was my mother. I called my mother "Martha," so did everyone else.

I was to be 4 years old in August and my brother was born in February. I didn't remember my mother being pregnant. My grandfather took me to the mid-wife's house that evening and I spent the night with her niece while the mid-wife went with my grandfather to deliver the baby. The next morning my grandfather came to take me home. It was a very sunny day. I was outside playing with the chickens. I said the chickens were singing "Swing Low."

When we arrived home my mother (Martha) was still in bed. I felt a little chilly so I sat in front of the fireplace to get warm. Soon I heard a baby cry and I said, "I hear a baby." Martha said, "Come here," and she showed me the baby. "This is your brother Henry." I asked, "Where did he come from?" and she said, "Mrs. Cates (the midwife) brought him here last night." I was very happy—now I would have someone to play with.

When I was about three-and-a-half years old I was left at the house to watch my grandmother who was bedridden. The other members of the family were working out in the fields and would come home for lunch at 12 o'clock and again at night. They taught me to give my grandmother her medication at 10 o'clock. My grandfather said, "When the hands of the clock is like this. . . it's time to give her the medicine."

My grandmother would talk to me when she was awake. One day I got in the chair to get her medication off the mantel, hit the clock and knocked it on the hearth. That broke the glass face of the clock.

I was so scared that I would get a spanking, I cleaned up the glass and took the clock to the chicken house and set it in there. This is where the chickens go to roost at night.

When my family came home from the field, the first place they looked was for the clock to see the time. My grandfather asked my grandmother, "Lara, where is the clock?"

When I heard this, I ran out of the house and brought the clock back. Crying, I said, "Here is the clock. I knocked it down when I was getting Mama's medicine. I didn't mean to do it."

My grandmother said, "Don't spank that child." My grandfather took me in his arms and hugged me and said, "That's all right, Cora."

My Mother

by Ethel McCullum
Tilden Towers II Senior Center

My mother is walking
down the road
thinking about the little
one inside
as the toad crosses her
path. She is making her way
to the spring
to get a pail of water.

There won't be any lead
in my belly
because my mother is drinking
nice cool spring water.
She stops to smell the daisies.

She smells the daffodils and
picks the violets
and listens to the singing birds
and watches the butterflies go by.
I should imagine she is holding on
to Beulah's hand—
my sister, on
her way to two years old.

Begonias

by Marie Capodieci
Mt. Carmel Center for Senior
Citizens

Three are planted
three more left
in box.

On cement walk
garden gloves spade
water can

Soil scattered
between box and
garden's edge

Four sparrows
settle their bodies
in the soil

With the flutter of wings
they clean themselves
in the dirt.

I Remember . . . (1900)

by Gertrude Lahey
Mt. Carmel Center for Senior Citizens

When I was eight years old I went to a German Catholic school and I had to walk eight blocks to get there. We went to Mass at 8:00, and before we started class we always said the Lord's Prayer. We had a Catechism class and when the sister would ask you a question in German you had to answer in English. One day, when she got to me, she asked it in English and I had to answer in German. I could not answer the whole question, so she hit me across the fingers two times and told me to go back, sit down and learn it. But I was so angry that I would not learn it. She called me up again and I told her I did not know it, so she hit me three times across the fingers again and it hurt so badly that I grabbed the rattan stick, lifted my leg, and broke it in two, then threw it back at her. I ran out of the room and went home without hat, rubbers and coat. I ran the eight blocks but it was snowing and I was almost frozen. My mother was so angry because the sister had hit me, so she took me out of that school and put me in an Irish school.

The Red Stockings

by Julius Sobel
Aging in America Senior Center

My house is a little barrio in the hill country in Mexico. We are very poor but we survive. Nobody in this little barrio has shoes. We all walk barefoot. For us it is very natural.

Something happened to me that almost ruined my life. An uncle who is rich died and left me a pair of red stockings. The people of the village all came to see my red stockings. They looked at and felt them and said, Jose, will you really wear them? This became for me a very big problem. If I wore them on my feet they would get dirty and wear out. What was I to do? I was going to hang them over the bed, but I was afraid someone would steal them. If my uncle had sent me his money I wouldn't have such problems. I finally realized that I couldn't keep the stockings. So I wrapped them up good and walked to the city and mailed them to my son who was going to college in the Estados Unidos. He will be happy to get them from me. What a relief it is for me that I don't have such a problem anymore. Back in my barrio the people greet me and they understand. I am happy again. You see, Dios is watching over me all the time.

A Special Place

by Julia Odierna
Mt. Carmel Center for Senior Citizens

It was a tropical island. Was this Paradise or Planet Earth? The sun had gone down in the West, the last rays cutting through the clouds that formed living figures of heavenly creatures in the sky. The beach was almost deserted and quiet except for the sound of the waves that broke the silver shore. The palm trees were quiet and majestic. The sand was warm under our feet and we could hear the seagulls flying over the water, singing goodbye to the day. I looked around for my mate—he was asleep on the sand. It had been a long day at the beach, we were both tired but we had to return to our home. Wake up, my dear. It is time to go. We left the beach behind, the sound of the waves, but not the feeling of belonging.

An excerpt from the novel *"Squirt"*

by Chris Belden

One summer morning Mrs. Dangle across the street ran out of her house and up and down the block wearing nothing but a girdle and a brassiere and the curlers in her hair. Up till that morning she had been just like my mom cleaning her house day after day while Mister Dangle worked at the quarry but there were times before her Crackup as my dad called it when I went over to borrow their hedge clippers or a stick of butter and I saw in Mrs. Dangle's face a hardness like it was about to crack like the wall above our toilet. Two months later when she came home from the Rest Farm nobody talked about her Little Accident as my mom called it but who could forget the sight of all two hundred pounds of her with those huge flopping boobs and arms waving and her big black hole of a mouth wide open in a nonstop shriek of the same word over and over again, Maytag! Maytag! Maytag! Maytag! Like everybody else I stood there watching partly terrified at seeing someone who had just the day before given me a bowlful of cherries from their backyard cherry tree suddenly go crazy but also thrilled at watching this huge half naked lady sprinting like an angry grizzly bear up and down the block.

I was in our front yard throwing a lime green frisbee against the house. If you threw it just right it would ricochet back to you just like those boomerangs from Australia. Plus it made a nice sound the hard plastic of the frisbee going *plonk* against the wood of the house. Then all of a sudden there was all this hollering from across the street and my mom came flying out of the front door wiping her hands on her yellow apron. That's when I saw Mrs. Dangle. Her skin was pink like the inside of a seashell they had down at school.

Get inside! my mom yelled but I ignored her which luckily for me she didn't notice while she had a pow wow with Mrs. Barton and Mrs. Olms out in the front yard. They talked quietly amongst themselves never taking their eyes off Mrs. Dangle who was still running up and down the sidewalk her voice growing hoarse now but her speed surprising for such a big lady. Mrs. Mancini joined the three women bringing with her a checkered blanket and they talked another minute before crossing the street and approaching Mrs. Dangle.

June, my mom called out, June it's okay calm down calm down. The others chanted the same thing, Please June take it easy, and Mrs.

Mancini who went swimming every day at the community center ran alongside Mrs. Dangle for a front yard length or two saying, June honey I want you to cover yourself up with this now, and she flung the blanket over Mrs. Dangle's shoulders where it hung for a few feet before falling to the sidewalk. Mrs. Dangle just kept running.

By now I was on the sidewalk watching. My mom looked over for a half second but she didn't say anything to me. She looked scared to death. One by one they tried keeping up with Mrs. Dangle and tossing the blanket and one by one they were outrun.

Tackle her, I thought. Chase her and tackle her from behind.

Finally Mrs. Dangle's legs started getting tired and her voice was just a scratchy whisper, May huh tag May huh tag, and her arms hung flabbily at her sides until in front of the Mancinis' house she fell onto her knees and sat back on her heels staring up at the clear blue sky and bawled like a baby. My mom reached her first and draped the blanket around her heaving shoulders covering her boobs and everything else so that Mrs. Dangle looked like a red and white checkered Indian kneeling beside the Mancinis' rhododendrons. There there June, the ladies whispered pulling her to her feet and walking her slowly back to her house.

Corny told me the doctors at the Rest Farm put electrodes on her head just like Frankenstein's monster but all I knew was that the next time I saw Mrs. Dangle her face wasn't hard anymore it was soft like putty and she never again gave me cherries from their backyard tree or waved from her porch when I rode by on my bike.

Sometimes I wondered if my mom was going to go crazy too. Sometimes I saw the same hardness in her face. Her wide eyes became like slits in an old fence surrounding a broken down building and her lips the same ones that kissed me so soft every night turned in on themselves as if she were chewing on them. Her nostrils flapped and even her hair which was usually soft and hung loose to her shoulders turned hard like a helmet.

This could happen at any time.

My mom did the same things just about every day of her life. I never noticed this until one rainy summer day when I was stuck in the house with nothing to do except follow her around watching. She got up at 7:30 and made coffee and eggs and bacon for my dad and some cereal with bananas for me and then after dad ran out of the house cursing the clock she fixed herself some toast before cleaning the plates and skillets and cups. About every ten minutes she let out a gigantic sigh as if she hadn't taken a breath since the last one. From there she made the beds and put in a load of laundry pausing to point out to me a stain on one of my dad's work shirts a stain she said never in a million years would come out.

Is it blood? I asked excited.

That doesn't look like blood to me, she said looking at it more closely. When I asked what it was she turned and marched back to the little laundry nook off the kitchen. Her face was hard then.

My mom never cleaned the house all at one time even though it was small. Instead she picked one room each day and went at it. After dusting she vacuumed and she scrubbed bare floors and she polished and waxed the wooden furniture. At noon she ironed my dad's shirts and watched soap operas clucking her tongue when a character did something stupid. Look at that fool, she said. Doesn't she know he's making a monkey outta her? For lunch she heated up some soup for me and made herself a sandwich that she ate between gasps over the bills she'd brought in from the mailbox. Then it was time to decide what to cook for dinner. It could only be one of a few things. Burgers or stew or shake & bake chicken or maybe meatloaf. It all depended on what was in the fridge. That day she settled on spaghetti because she'd bought two jars of sauce at half price at the A & P and because it was Grandma's favorite.

Grandma was supposed to be staying with Uncle Roach but she was coming over for dinner and to spend the night with us because Roach was having his house bombed for bugs. Whenever Grandma came over my dad usually stopped by Red's Bar after work and drank a few beers to prepare for the Old Bat as he called her and that night he missed supper completely and still hadn't called or shown up at 9:00. My mom was tight lipped with worry but Grandma who'd had a few shots of bourbon babbled on and on about her no-good son-in-law out with other no-good men not having the decency to come home to their families for supper. My mom was quiet but her face became harder and harder her fingers jerking quickly as she needlepointed a pillowcase for a second cousin who was getting married to a doctor down in Florida. There was a little yellow house and a green lawn and a white dog beside a tree.

We were watching TV when dad finally showed up his shirt untucked his hair wild his eyes all shot with blood. My mom ignored him when he stumbled to his chair mumbling something about how he lost track of time but Grandma gave him her hairy eyeball routine the one that could peel paint off a statue.

I sure am hungry, he said licking his pasty lips. I could eat *two* horses!

Mom didn't even look up from the pillowcase. What's for supper? my dad asked and Grandma said, You'd know if you'da been here. Dad's eyes became squinty and he asked if there was any leftovers of the food he worked his butt off all week to buy us.

You got feet, Grandma said, and you know where the fridge is located.

When my dad was in his vinyl easy chair he did not like to get up unless it was to go to the bathroom and never ever did he get up to grab himself a bite to eat. That was a woman's work. He looked away from grandma's burning eyes and told my mom to fetch him some chow. Her fingers hesitated at the needlepoint but she managed to ignore his order. Grandma beamed.

All right, he said turning to me. Go get me some dinner boy. I stood up but my mom said without lifting her face, Sit down.

What did you say? my dad asked her.

I'll get it, she said. Just keep your pants on.

She set down the needlepoint frame and went into the kitchen. Dad grinned at Grandma as if saying, I won this one, but her face just grew meaner. My Mom came back with a bowl of cold spaghetti piled high and a can of beer and she set it in dad's lap and returned to the couch all without once looking him in the eye. Grandma's liver spotted hands got more and more fidgety in her lap as my dad chewed and drank and belched and finally she stood up making a big show of it with gasps and grunts and hobbled towards the bedroom. Dad watched her go and waved a fork like it was a baton in time to her limp until she disappeared into my bedroom which was where she slept when she stayed with us.

My mom didn't hardly move and her face stayed hard even during her favorite TV show which my dad thought was so funny he blew a swallow of beer through his nose. She never said anything she just sat at her spot on the couch needlepointing. When the show was over she picked up her needlepoint frame and marched into their bedroom and slammed the door behind her.

What's *her* problem? my dad asked though I could tell he didn't expect me to answer. He told me to go get him another brewski and after that I lay under my blanket on the couch with my eyes screwed shut but wide awake listening to the audience laughter from the TV shows and from somewhere else the sound of crying.

Ronaldo V. Wilson attended the University of California, Berkeley, and received his MA in Creative Writing at New York University, where he completed his first volume of poetry, "*open letter to the con edison man near my body.*" He has performed at Joseph Papp's Public Theatre, the Knitting Factory and the Nuyorican Poets' Cafe. With WritersCorps, he held poetry workshops at the Mosaic Community Center in the South Bronx.

Photo by Dallas Bauman, III

I write in order to construct the world around me in a way that I think is digestible. The more I live and write, the divisions between the two become nonexistent. I think it's become harder to live as a writer. I write poetry because I have a lot of fun with it, and it's a good way to shorthand my existence. I find I have a talent for encapsulating moments, for summing things up, and from there I ask myself, how do I turn this into a poem? So for me, it's also a question of why I am writing a particular piece, or, addressing a particular issue in the world. Then I stretch it, figure every little intricacy to explain the event, give it context and shape.

I grew up with a lot of science—my brother's an engineer, my father's an electronics technician—so there was always a figurative language to discuss the world. My brother started reading when he was about three, so by the time he was seven, and I was four, he was reading science fiction novels, and that developed into our play— much of which was me being terrified. He had me believing in monsters until I was 10 or 11. He made me believe in these things, because he was very sophisticated, in terms of being able to understand and present this material, and terrify me with it. So it was with that precision that I developed a particular world view, where everything is very shaky and very fantastic. I was also encouraged to write at an early age because I could articulate what I saw—like believing there were people inside my pencil.

What was hardest for me with my students in WritersCorps was to see—not a lack of imagination, but a lack of the ability to articulate that imagination through the creative process. That was the challenge. In terms of how it's affected my own writing, my strongest poems—the scarecrow poems—have to do with seeing things that weren't particularly there—this kind of yearning, this undercurrent that I find in the Bronx, this absence of life under the garbage—and that really interests me. Ironically, those poems weren't that accessible to my students. What did work were poems that were more family-centered, in a more common language.

I did have success with my workshops, but I didn't know it until later. I realized that what I had tapped into was that feeling of yearning. I'd bring in work by Sharon Olds, Marilyn Nelson Waniek, love poems, poems about a sense of yearning, a desperation to find out where center is. In many ways that did come across. My assignments were fun, too. I took them to junk yards and lots where there was nothing but garbage. I would do persona poems, and these personas were dirty toilets and cigarette wrappers. Once they had a context for their yearning, it was amazing what they came up with. Of course the stories from these kids and their families are incredible. One of my students told me, in the midst of a conversation, that his grandmother was stabbed to death, that they found her body in the elevator. So any button you press is a dangerous one.

In many ways the mission of WritersCorps is up for grabs. Ideally it's having a certain number of artists going into the community and helping people generate work, and hoping that work evolves. For me it wasn't that easy or clear-cut. How do you bring an artist into the community? How do you say, look there's this living artist, we need to develop an identity, an audience, to show that this person is a viable figure who can help, who's going to make something happen? How do we create niches for artists, make them a normal part of a community, so that they are just as much the reality as a grandmother being stabbed in an elevator? I guess it's about possibilities.

Garrett Hongo says if we don't have poets, we don't have people who can give us another history, an alternative to the dominant forms, such as the media. It's healthy for writers to be in a position where they can take language and place it in an exact way, and move people, events. Ngugi Wa Thiongo says dreaming is the exact process of writing, that there are these foreign elements that writers put together that don't make sense. Writing doesn't necessarily have to make sense—just the way dreams don't. We need that kind of record, especially in America, where the English language is constantly changing, to articulate in ways that aren't always about power or money, but more about our natural way of living. The act of making things linear is very silencing. We need writers to constantly offset this tendency to make everything concrete. That's the good thing about WritersCorps, that I can say that to my students. Who else is going to tell them that? Their teachers aren't; it's not their concern.

*poems from the Mosaic Community Center
AfterSchool Writers' Club*

Brown Paper Bag
by Shaquan B.

I was used in the store. Then a customer came. He used me for holding some things that he purchased like ice cream and juice. When they put it in me I felt cold I was so cold and I was wet. Then after they finished they threw me in the street. A car drove over me. I felt dirty. I had wet stains from the rain. I was a brown beautiful paper bag before.

I feel out/I feel in the Street
by Juan O.

People,

Building

Music
Beach

The air
The flower
I feel cool
I feel out\I feel in the street

Cigarette Box
by Sabrina R.

One day Emily was smoking. Then the next day she finished with me and I was going down to the dust. I was lonely and I was feeling dirt, old, nasty, ran on by a big foot. I wish that Emily would not finish with me I miss her. The world feels so sad. 2 weeks later I died and my memory stayed there forever and body.

Being Sad
by Elizabeth R.

I feel sad when my father's niece
Danora died, because she had leukemia.
I feel sad when my cousin died in birth
And I feel sad when my uncle
died in a fire. I have feelings
inside but I don't want to let them out but this time
I have to show people how I feel.
Now since part of my family died I think I will lose them all
because my mother has heart murmurs and she
was very sick these weeks.

The Water Fountain
by Obencio E.

It makes noise and the
water moves and it's very
cold. The noise sounds like somebody
whistling and it reminds me like
a waterfall.
What I see is water that is falling and it looks
like a water in a big river
in a white pond.
It makes me feel good because I like river.
I like ponds.

This Morning I Woke Up With My Eyes Closed
by Evelyn D.

This morning I woke up with my eyes closed.
What a shock it was to see the world within.
I left the cave, the spiders followed.
So into the pocket they went. I hopped on my
hearse and off to work I went.
My job is exciting. I wear white I cut
off tongues of those who lie. I cut it &
I chop it to pieces then I mix it and serve it.
After a hard day of cutting tongues,
I punch out my boss, and go directly to the meat market.
Sell some freshly cut gossip tongue for the next day.
During the late night I shower with mud and dry my
self with sand paper. I perfume myself with spit and off I go
to my bed of hot coal.

If You Mean It

by Sandra C.

Where can I go, what must
I do?
To find a love that's deep, and wet
and true?
I've heard the words so many times
before
Words un-meant true lies false meanings
and more
In my bed he creeps into at night
with thoughts of lust and words so
sweet
Caressing my naked body underneath the
silky sheet
the clock ticked hours away as my
body awaited his touch,
now he's arrived with candies & flowers,
but the love's not much,
I can feel the lies when my hair he
strokes
though my sexual desires he continuously
provokes
So I give into his insincere and lustful
ways

In the hope my love will bring better nights
and hopeful days.
Often I wonder how could my life
turn out to be,
Full of lies, deceits and traps
instead of Free.
How could someone say what they do not mean
or show what they do not feel
without not counting the hearts
they tend to steal
Sometimes I wish my ears were
deaf, to all the words, my heart can
hear,
for then I'd be hard and cruel and never
shed a tear
then again I stop and wonder, is this the price I pay
for choosing a male to love,
and turning out
gay,
yes my name is Victor and it's my life
my parents blame it all on me for not
having chosen a wife,
But how unhappy my life would be
had I never met my friend Eddie.

Color Memories
by Milagros C.

Mama from a picture
hiding from the sun under her umbrella
her pale white fragile body
her big brown eyes
full red lips
a smile that we all have
shiny long white hair
combed in a bun
thin strong arms
not quite smooth hands
from milking cows to embroider hankies
she was a hard working woman
she wore a simple checkered colorful dress
she had sewed herself
her nicely shaped legs
with a few varicose veins
from standing all day
in silky skin-tone stockings
and old fashioned black medium heel shoes

poems from
"open letter to the con edison man near my body"
by Ronaldo V. Wilson

note to those who may devour me

be warned of my orange poison
argyle socks my matching scarf
beware of my red eyes rank
breath
don't try   to swallow me

you will swell
heavy secretions
will form in your mouth
you cannot eat my matted hair
my united states of america flag
thematic
    sunglasses
caustic
    the neon stripe flashing
        under my fatigues

i've learned to survive
without wings   beak
i don't hunt
my teeth are dulled and flat
i don't own
raising vertebrae
dangerous fins
camouflage ability
or a shell

but if you do
corner me
i will bite
aiming
 for your
        eyes

48

for ceo
by Ronaldo V. Wilson

not even the pineapples know
or the watermelon
wedges or even the whole parts
the zig zag stitches
not even the elastic
in your favorite tube top knows
not even your daddy   knows
about the fire or the cherry
no one knows
why your arms fling
like blades
of a propeller
broken off their joints
no one in here can save you
not even the man behind you
this man next to your daddy
the man who owns the cigarette
the owner of fire
the owner of the cherry
burning in your back
not even he can save you
from his own fire   from his cherry
pin point white hot
in the pineapples and watermelon
in the zig zag stitches
in the skin between your
shoulder blades
your daddy   searches
for your screaming
your propeller frenzy
your running in place
your daddy swats and rough
brushing
but the cherry is still
burning   you
before it crumbles into ash
before it's ash on the tile of the lobby

the cherry's done
its melting
of your skin
your favorite tube top
is stretched
into frowns
where your daddy pulled
he lifts you over his shoulder
you still
trying to run in place
and the man's real sorry about
burning you
realizes how careless
his fire
he say   *if this doesn't get me to quit*

pearl

by Ronaldo V. Wilson

near the back of a museum
in historical boston
rests a bloodied shred of a minute man's
killed shirt sealed under glass
it's preserved with a note
says *he was shot dead mid battle at bunker hill*

i'm all for the preservation of these
stained snippets from the uniforms of soldiers
glass cases and placards detailing their dying

pearl strays barefoot up from the underground
out sixth avenue and forty eighth street
in manhattan
the hot wet in the air weighs
her trash bag moo moo down
plastic creases deep
around the opening she's torn
for her pregnant
stomach

and who will resurrect a shrine
for a piece of pearl's bag
plastic or her skin?
the sweat slicked glob cut from her belly
where it bulges out the bag
like an immense keloid
blood cells and baby tissue   quivering

what hero will return? —
to this historical museum
pearl's skin in hand

who will call her uniform? soldier?

what hero is willing to lay
her flesh
over this old
blood?

51

scarecrow
by Ronaldo Wilson

everyday i pass you   your body

a mess of straw   knee caps exploding
your pillow case pants
blooming out into
the oil wreck off the
curb
last night   someone ripped out your back
today a crystal burden of hailstones   this freezing

and broken bottles pushing up into your neck
bed springs from old couch backs
shanks of metal springs through your legs

someone has tugged off   your head
removed   your eyes

i want to mend them   two green felt patches to your face
again
find rope   now
knot your neck to your head

every day a new   dying
you speak to me
of your seeing
of the rollings over the same balls of clouds
the same grey boiling   of the sky above you
your boots   hanging in the telephone wires
your sweater tangled in the fence

you long for your field   of tire hulls   charred radiators the
calls from the burned out windows of high rises dead washing
machines
the quickness of starving squirrels
 wild skinny cat strays
 silent   bombed out   dogs

you need plywood to be propped upon
someone to clean your ragged pants
  pull the glass from your neck

you tell me you dream
in rows of corn
simple wheat fields
crows and of guarding
and of the sun
pushing on your back
and how you want most   to be warm

Willard Cook is a fiction writer and poet, with an MA from New York University and an MFA from Vermont College. A former reporter for UPI, he is currently adjunct professor at Marymount Manhattan College. His stories and poems have appeared in *"The New York Times," "Pleiades," "Chimera,"* and others. As a Bronx WritersCorps member, he was writer-in-residence at H.E.L.P. Bronx.

Photo by Gary Miller

I'm a writer in order to express myself. I started writing journals in order to process a lot of my emotions, and wrote poetry for a long time. I got into fiction because I like to write stories—stories were a way of looking at life. I always did terribly in English during school, and the worse I did the more determined I was to overcome my failures. I like the preciseness of writing. Trying to express myself in words takes a lot more discipline for me than other art forms. In high school I did a lot of painting and I think that it came very naturally to me. Again, it's a matter of going for the more challenging form.

There are times when I want to put down my pen and not write anymore. Writing has been very powerful for me—to express the shadow realm, the truths in my life that I can't express elsewhere. In journals I always want to tell the truth about my life, and yet in life, I'd rather tell lies. Fiction tells an even deeper truth than journals, because it allows me to put on a mask. It's the old saying, "When you're writing fiction, tell the truth, and when you're writing the truth, tell lies."

We live our lives like stories, and writing for me reinforces that. I get up in the morning, and each day is a different story. Narrative is a unique way to understand our lives. When Dan Rather goes on the evening news, for instance, he's got his narratives about what's happening in America. We all share stories. We share the O.J. Simpson trial—that's a powerful and sad story. It's a way in which people can connect on a deep level. There's a strong human thirst for understanding life through the story, and that's the role of writing—to capture that, and pass it along.

WritersCorps fulfills a lot of needs for me. I teach in college, and I find college a very closed environment. It's almost like a mutual admiration society. I know how to teach the class, I know how to press the buttons, I know how to "inspire" the students, but there's less of a challenge there for me because I'm teaching highly educated people. In academia, people are trying to show off— "My story's better than your story" instead of simply "I have an interesting story here, my story is a gift." This kind of hot dog one-upmanship in academia is very troubling to me.

WritersCorps has allowed me to go outside that small circle, and reach out to different populations that have pretty fantastic stories. It's challenged me to get them to tell those stories. I work with homeless people, and it's a very transient population. Some days I go in and nobody's there, other days I go in and there's six women and two screaming babies. It's a difficult situation, but in many ways, it mirrors my own creative process. Some days you sit down at the typewriter and think, "Why the hell am I doing this?"

The same thing happens when I go in to teach the homeless women with their screaming babies, and it's complete chaos. I ask myself, "Why am I doing this?" But then there's those days when you go in and you really connect. It's much closer to the chaos of existence, and to me that's what fiction tries to capture. There's greater risk, greater reward. WritersCorps has allowed me to identify myself as a writer, whereas in academia I identify myself as a teacher.

I don't know what effect this has on society. I know it's important that we express ourselves, and that I've connected on a meaningful level; I know that these women are writing, that they're starting to express themselves in powerful ways. There's probably two or three people who have become writers since I've been there. They've gone from a place of being very shut down, to a place of expressing themselves through writing.

Where that writing will take them, I don't know. I'm reluctant to say that writing is good for the community. I think it's one way in which people connect. That's what it's about—connecting with other human beings—and writing is just the way we've done it.

from H.E.L.P. Bronx

Shattered Dreams

by Rita W.

One way my dream was shattered was when I had to come and live in a shelter with my kids. I came to H.E.L.P. Bronx in September of '94. I became so shattered that I thought my world was falling apart. My mother did not appreciate me coming to a shelter. I had to find out the hard way. It is all different kinds of people in shelters throughout New York City. I wish to God that when I get out of this shelter I will not have to go to another one. Hopefully I will get an apartment and make my dream a reality. Because if I turn back my life would be shattered all over again. Shattered dreams hurts one feeling very much. Don't dream about what you want to become, just do it. All it takes is for you to go forward not backwards, keep looking ahead to the dream and make it come true. If you look back you will get lost in the world, and never will your dream come true. Shattered dreams are painful and oppressive. I wouldn't really want to dream I would try to make it happen.

I feel neglected now because I am living in a shelter and it seems like my family is distantly away from me forever. I am sometimes dazzled in distress. Most of the time I wonder if they still love me. When I had my phone in, my family did not call me. Once in a while the phone would ring and it would be a family member. I can't imagine how cruel and evil family can be. I feel if I was not living in a shelter my family would look at me in a better perspective. I know my life would be more exciting and over all well pleased. It is very boring that's why I go to school and try to learn something, so I can get ahead in life and not be just another sitter for the rest of my life.

I Remember

by Rita W.

I remember I was living with my mother in a small room with my kids. My mother had lost the house and she got a room in another house on the same block. We stayed in the room with her. My kids had to sleep on the couch. She would sleep in a chair and I would try to squeeze in on the couch. It was so frustrating to live in that house. I had to buy food out everyday. I had to spend most of my money and then some. Living in that room was crowded and very uncomfortable. We had to heat water to take a bath and wash our hair. I am so glad that I moved out of that room. My kids and I were planning to leave, but we had to wait, because my husband was vicious at that time. Now I can thank God that I have a better place to rest my head. Some people think shelters are bad, but if they go and live in some places they will be saying that they would rather live in a nice shelter. My mother would not move because she loves that block. I would go and visit her and I would be totally disgusted seeing her living like that. I would tell her won't you look for a better place on that block.

Homelessness
by Magda C.

What I feel about being homeless is that there are degrees of homelessness, just like there are different social classes. If I were to categorize them I would say that the first is being without a home. This is the worst—no shelter, no money and no hope. Second is where a homeless person has a little money, lives in a shelter and is trying their damnedest to survive. Then there is the third where I am in decent and clean temporary housing, with some money and most importantly the hope of getting an apartment soon.

All these stages have one thing in common: being without a home. I never fully appreciated what I had until I lost it. I never thought of having to live in a temporary shelter, nor did I imagine it as a clean or decent place to live. I thought of a shelter as a place of chaos. Dirty, scary and dangerous people living on top of each other. I felt it would be unsafe.

I remember the first time I heard the word shelter mentioned in the reference to my life. For about a year I was looking for an apartment and I was getting desperate and frankly so was my landlady. Finally she got fed up and told me that she thought it would be best if I went to a shelter. I choked when I heard her say that. I became depressed, angry and scared all at once, but the feeling that dominated was fear—fear of being put in a room with my three children with crazy, drunk and belligerent people. People I would have nothing in common with.

After all, I am Magda, the only daughter of a doting family and the first grandchild. Imagine me, who had always loved school and books and was always proud of my high school diploma, being homeless. Being homeless, I thought, was not me. I don't drink, I don't do drugs. Most of all I had a family. Shelters were for derelicts. I was smug and self-righteous. The young are always so full of themselves and I was no different. I thought I knew it all.

First of all, now that I am homeless, I have had to dispel the common stereotype and realize that homeless people are from many different backgrounds, but that it is mostly about people who are in desperate situations and have nowhere to turn. Shelters are for people who have nowhere to turn. Some become homeless because they have lost their jobs and have no other means to support themselves. Some leave their homes because they are in abusive relationships and their only way out is to seek shelter. Others are here because they have a substance abuse problem and are unable to keep a job while seeking treatment.

Just like the world is made up of different people with different backgrounds so are the homeless. Homelessness doesn't equal drunk. Homelessness doesn't equal lazy. Homelessness doesn't equal drug addict. For me, it means a 25 year old woman who at age 19 didn't know any better, didn't know how to manage her life and got herself in a whole heap of trouble, but who is trying damn hard to straighten her life out.

I Miss Him

by Lenasha C.

I woke up this morning and I looked out the window and I thought of my ex-husband. It made me feel sad I missed him so much. I miss having him around to talk to. I don't know. I still don't think I want him around. He beat me up one time and my eye swelled up like a plum. I told him to get the fuck out of my life. But even with all the messed up shit he did to me I still want him back.

Home

by Derrek S.

Home is three gray pigeons sitting on a wall
Home is the siren of a fire engine screaming
at six o'clock in the morning
Home is chilling out on Saturday night and watching TV
Home is a full moon on a cold clear night
Home is a glass of water
Home is being homeless
Home is the way my grandmother used to smile
Home is three crackheads and the hooker
buggin out on my corner
Home here in America is AIDS, movie stars
and the man I saw get shot on my seventh birthday.

Dreaming

by Keema W.

I am dreaming.
In my heart
are three rivers
that flow through
these Bronx streets
death
sex
& smiling children.

Geography
(An Excerpt)

by Willard Cook

At three o'clock Macy met Lena in the school parking lot and as they were weaving their way through the cars Macy said her mother had fainted again and they had taken her to North Adams General Hospital. Her mother collapsed in the frozen food section of the Cub Food's Warehouse when she imagined she saw Max, her ex-boyfriend, the one who had cut her in the throat with a hunting knife almost five years ago now.

"She had fainting spells all over the place back then," Macy said, stepping over an old wooden railroad tie on the periphery of the parking lot.

"I bet you were scared stiff," Lena said, trailing along behind her.

"It didn't bother me at all."

Macy was seven when the assault happened, and Buck, her brother, was almost three. Macy doesn't remember much about how Max came into her mother's life, but she remembers his imposing height, his peppery hair and tired gray eyes. Macy told her Mom she thought he was unpredictable, sometimes angry, sometimes kind, and other times gloomy beyond belief. Her Mom defended her new boyfriend: "Just be patient. He's got a good heart."

Macy had never seen the attack, but whenever she was asked about it she pretended she had seen the whole thing. She liked to embellish the story with gory details to create authenticity. She said that blood got all over the hood of the car, which was true, but Macy scarcely saw any of it. She was still in the North Adams K-Mart when it happened. Her Mom had refused to buy her a bottle of three dollar blue-sparkled fingernail polish, so Macy deliberately strayed into the TV section. She was hypnotized by a close-up of red raspberry puckered lips. There were twenty simultaneous images that impressed her. She wanted her lips to be sexy like that. A skinny salesman with a hard angular face and suspicious eyes watched Macy as she surveyed the different televisions. She averted her eyes trying to look like she had somewhere to go. She sauntered off down through a row of toasters, microwave ovens and coffee machines puckering her own lips in the shiny reflection of toasters. She anticipated that her mother was going to grab her by the arm and give her a lecture about the dangers of being kidnapped.

Outside in the parking lot Macy looked up at the overcast New England sky and still felt resentment about the fingernail polish. She heard a woman shrieking hysterically. It sounded like her mother's voice, but it couldn't be, she thought. Macy ran toward the sound, but a man stopped her — grabbed her arm before she could get to her screaming mother. Macy struggled, she caught a glimpse of her mother, and there was blood all down her chin and neck and on her Mickey Mouse sweat shirt. She didn't believe what she had seen. After that day, Macy's life turned into a roller coaster ride of her mother's ups and downs, stops and starts, and finally a descent into what the doctors would call clinical depression.

Months later, Macy would find herself wondering how the assault had happened so fast. How could her mother have been assaulted in broad daylight? She wondered what would have happened if she hadn't wandered away. What if she had done what she was supposed to?

The judge sentenced Max, the ex-boyfriend, to a mental hospital in Springfield, but there was no place on earth that her mother would feel safe. Max was everywhere in their lives. Macy could see that in her mother's eyes, and just when the whole thing seemed to be getting better, that's when her mother fell apart.

Macy and Lena walked side by side and Macy stopped and set her book bag on the sidewalk in front of the old stone Catholic Church where Lena and her family went on Sundays. She had to check for her geography book. She looked up at the church. It had been built in 1909 when the city was full of shoe factories. She liked the weathered look of the gray stone, the large carved oak doors, the silver crack in the steeple, but most of all she liked the pure silence on the inside of the church — almost as if God himself were there. In that silence she felt calm; safe from her mother and safe from Max. Once she had asked her mother if she could go to the Catholic church with Lena's family. She wanted to go to church and pray to God to have a family like Lena's, but her mother ignored her. She said there was too much to be done around the house on Sundays, though they always seemed to sit on her mother's bed and watch afternoon movies. Macy intently searched her green canvas book bag for her geography book. She liked having to pinpoint far away places like Timor, Bali, Waingapu, and imagine what it would be like to live there. She wanted to go to one of those far away places someday.

Maybe one of the islands in Polynesia. She had read that when someone got sick everybody who lived in the village helped out by bringing gifts, doing the daily chores and comforting the family. When she felt the thick paperback textbook, she let out a sigh of relief. She had come to know her geography book well and felt she could look up just about any information she needed.

Macy studied local maps, too. Being able to locate where she was gave her a sense of security. She had made a brightly colored detailed map of the immediate neighborhood and Scotch taped it to her bedroom wall. She knew the quickest route to the police station and had even walked the seven blocks.

Macy stood up, put her book bag over her shoulder. She wanted Lena to understand.

"The doctor said we have to blank the really horrible stuff out and that's what Mom was doing when she fainted."

"I saw a dog get run over by a car once. God, it was gross. He was all smushed, but I never blanked it out," Lena said.

"No, it would only happen if somebody close to you like your Mom or Dad died right in front of you and you had to watch the whole thing. He told this story about these Cambodians who went blind from looking at too many people getting blown to pieces by bombs. Their brains couldn't take it anymore."

"Well, people aren't being blown up around here," Lena said.

"No, but my Mom is still blanking out. She doesn't want to see what she has seen again, so she faints instead."

The man Macy's mother saw yesterday in the frozen food section looked similar because of his thick brown mustache, but, unlike Max, this man was short and fat. He had a large belly hidden beneath a bright yellow t-shirt, and curly brown hair coming out from the sides of a light blue baseball cap. When Macy's mother fainted the man immediately came over to help. He screamed at the stock boy to call an ambulance. The rest of the story was sort of a blur and Macy really didn't feel like telling it because this fainting spell felt the same as it did when her mother came home the first time from the hospital with the 27 stitches in her throat. Macy didn't like to talk about it much, only enough to get Lena's sympathy.

Macy moved over to the edge of the sidewalk and ran her finger along the door of a dusty black Buick that had a dent in the driver's side door just like her Mom's old Chevette. That car vibrated and shook like an earthquake every time the car hit a bump or a pothole.

The rattling got even worse the night after Max kicked the dent in the door. She was in her room playing with her dolls when she heard a loud and angry voice from the kitchen. Was that Max? Macy wondered. The voice repeated, but this time it sounded like an explosion.

"You fucked him, didn't you?" She heard something — maybe a dish — fall and break and then a snarl like a badger. Had this happened before? Macy sat on the edge of her bed, frozen, her doll tightly in hand, looking into her doll house, wondering if her mother would still be able to make the miniature curtains she had promised. She heard, but she didn't hear, she didn't want to hear, she wasn't supposed to hear: the sound of her mother being beaten. Macy's body was there on the bed, but some part of her retreated into her closet, shutting the door away from the sound of the beating. She went where no one could get her. When the beating dwindled she heard the loud slap of the kitchen door shutting. She got up from her bed, somnambulant, and went to the window and watched Max. He was kicking the door of her mother's car with his big black motorcycle boots, kicking it endlessly like the car was alive and he was going to kill it. Finally, exhausted, he stumbled down the driveway. After he left, Macy seemed to come alive again.

She ran downstairs and locked the kitchen door. Her mother was doubled over on the floor, panting like a dog and gripping her stomach. Macy knelt down, officious and doctor-like, put her hand on her mother's shoulder. Her mother let out a growl of pain. Her lip was fat and bleeding. Even at eight years old Macy knew precisely what to do. She had to learn how to take care of Buck and she had even brought her mother lots of tea one day when she was sick in bed. She went immediately to the bathroom and ran cold water on a washcloth, squeezed it until it was damp, then returned to the kitchen where her mother was now sitting upright. Macy took the cool terry cloth and pressed it tenderly against the fat lip. As she did this her mother looked at her and said,

"Everything is going to be okay, sweetheart."

Now when Macy thinks back to this time she feels quite sure that her mother did something to provoke Max into such a rage. She remembers one breezy summer afternoon when she was sitting on the kitchen floor eating Oreos, drinking milk and looking at a brightly colored picture book of Africa when a man pressed his face against the screen door and asked, "Your Mom here?" The man was younger than her Mom. Her mother was just out of the shower,

64

bright and perky. Macy remembers the man was handsome. She remembers how the man squeezed her mother's hand and kissed her. It was a wet sensuous kiss, one that Macy pretended she didn't see.

She remembers the hurried feeling of her younger years — her mother constantly pushing to go here or there or do this or that. She was always on the move, always in a rush, always trying to get somewhere. She could never sit still, but since the attack her mother's body has had to slow down, and yet her mind is still scheming to bust lose and run; from Max; from her children; from that committee of voices in her head.

Macy can still hear the rage in Max's voice. She hears it loud and clear almost as if it were her own voice screaming at her mother, but beyond the voice are images that won't go away. She sees her doll house, the shattered plate, and her mother folded over on the kitchen floor. All of these images swirl in her head like little dust storms, but nothing fits or settles the way she would like. She wants to fix her mother's sickness. She prays that her mother will be safe, that things will be okay like they are in Lena's family.

As they walk along, Macy looks at Lena's long blonde hair and new blue overcoat. She wishes she had both. She wishes she could be Lena growing up with a real mother and real father, but deep down she knows this will never happen and she is going to have to look after her baby brother Buck. She wants to tell Lena about last week when she warmed a can of Spaghetti O's, and made peanut butter and butter sandwiches because her mother never came home. She and Buck watched TV and ate dinner. When Macy answered the phone her mother's voice sounded far away like she was way out in the desert somewhere near Arizona where her cousins lived. She told Macy she had run out of gas on the highway, but Macy knew it was a fainting spell. She knew her mother was sick again and she hated her mother for being that way.

Jennifer Webster graduated from St. Lawrence University in 1993 with a Bachelor of Arts in Anthropology. She began writing fiction at the age of 12. Currently, she is attending the University of Oregon to pursue a Master of Arts in International Development. As a member of WritersCorps she worked with the Mosholu Preservation Corporation.

Photo by Wayne Providence

I really don't define myself as a writer in terms of a profession. I just happen to enjoy writing. That's one of my main problems at the moment—that I don't have a definition for myself that's clear-cut. I will say I hope to be doing community service for the rest of my life.

I like the idea of teaching kids the basic skills of writing, how to read and write, by teaching poetry. I thought it would be fun. I think it's really important that people learn how to express themselves. A lot of the problems that inner city people have are exacerbated by the fact that they don't express themselves—they don't write to their congressmen and their newspaper editors—they're not heard because they're not speaking out in the places where they need to be heard.

My experience with WritersCorps reinforced my own desire to work in community service. In the northwest Bronx there are a lot of community-based organizations working toward improving the neighborhoods. I liked the general atmosphere and met a lot of people who were genuinely excited about what was going on in their community.

I worked with the vice president of Mosholu Preservation Corporation, whose job was to make the neighborhood better. He was so supportive and enthusiastic. I'd be working with middle school kids on their school newspaper and little things would happen—like the newspaper would get a new column and he'd get really excited, because there was a time when there was no newspaper. Talking with him I learned how much work it takes to start with a community that's dying and get people to notice that it does have life. That got me excited and I started thinking about what I could do to help rebuild my own community.

When I first applied to WritersCorps I thought it was basically a literacy program—that through creative writing we would teach basic reading and writing skills. As it turned out, my site was more of a community development project. I had to get teens from the community to care about creative writing and to produce work. It took a long time to get anything started.

In some ways I don't think my project ever started to click. It took me many weeks just to lay the groundwork. Then a lot happened at once. I would have teens showing up for the teen workshop, and other kids showing up for the library workshop. At the same time, the kids at the middle school were working on their group story for the next issue of the newspaper.

I think my biggest accomplishment was laying the groundwork for whoever comes to that site next year. The library is pretty excited

68

about continuing the poetry workshop which I started, open to kids of all ages. Initially, the library program was only supposed to last four weeks. After the fourth week, however, we all said, why don't we meet next week? We kept meeting on a weekly basis for the next four months.

Toward the end of the program we had lots going on. We had a poetry reading for the kids at the library, where I also invited community members to read from their own manuscripts. People from the community were excited about the opportunity to read, and also to see the kids interested in this type of activity. We also published a literary journal through the local newspaper—a four-page insert. That was pretty exciting for the kids, to see their work out in the community. Writing allows people to see things as other people see them. It helps everyone to have a better perspective when they read works by others.

I didn't have time to do much writing of my own during the program, but I expect I'll continue my writing even as I pursue other careers. If there's one writer who's work I truly admire it's Orson Scott Card, a fantasy and science fiction writer. If I could ever write a story remotely close to the way he writes a story—I'll die happy.

Community service is important because that's the way life was meant to be—if you live in a community you should be involved in it. I grew up in a place where I don't even know my neighbors. I think that's one of the biggest problems we face today—communities are so fragmented that they're practically dysfunctional. Community building has got to become a major social issue for this country to mend.

The Park
by Rebecca S.

I am sitting on a park bench
but it doesn't seem like a park.
It has buildings and highways all around it.
There is only one tree in this park.
There is only one swing.
There is only one slide.
It is not the park I remember.
When I used to come with my mom and dad,
There were no highways
Or buildings
It was pretty great.
But now look at it,
It's polluted and horrible.
Children can't come here,
This isn't a park, it's a junk yard.
Just a junk yard.
What a shame,
Oh what a shame.
I wish it would change.
The park is like my life,
A black pit of nothing.
Nobody's happy,
Everyone's sad.
What a park...
The park.

Hard Times
by Danielle W.

I look out my bedroom window and all I see is people who are in a rush. Tall buildings. Lights. Drug Dealers. Homeless people. My life can become difficult and complicated to deal with. It's hard to wake up in the morning and think of my life as simple and great. I'm not very in touch with my family. They live in a great paradise, full of palm trees and colorful evening skies. I don't care about material things. Only things that matter, things that are happening out there. I think I would like to move some-where else but I can't it's too late. But I don't think my life is sad. I do have a life, a best friend, a pet. The average stuff. But something is missing. Maybe it's happiness. But I know some people are in garbage—dumps. So I thank the Lord.

Baby Days
by Danielle W.

I am a baby entering the world
Everything is nice and pretty and new
Like when snow is falling then when it falls it's black
  and wet
I feel empty in my heart
But when I grow up my heart will fill
  with love and cheer.
I have a fear that if I'm blessed with something bad
I will always be alone and sad.
I'll lay against my bed
And when I'm awakened
I'll feel nice and fresh.
In my dreams I dream of a river floating
  with love and care
And my father and mother belong there
I look at a photograph that's on the ground
It's like looking at a mirror
Maybe that's my twin
I can't wait to be a kid
I'll love it so much
But it will never, ever compare, then and now.

Scream Something

by Stephen W.

Your indifference burns me twice more
than any hate you throw at me
For if you hate, you notice,
think about that which is unpleasing,
And a passion burns

You used to hate, long ago
Now you wouldn't waste the spittle
Am I not worthy of even
your screams and swears?

The heartfelt curses and oaths of loathe
would comfort me, a blanket
for a sleeping soul
longing to be awakened

But no, you are the bored sales clerk
And I only a child
And all we have are whispers
of monotony, and bitter silence
all your anger gone
like ghosts from covered graves

Hate and mock me
but I shall not drown
in horrid apathy

I still care
I still care
I hate you

Big Red Machine With White Letters
Thomas B.

Whisk me away from
my day of toil and trouble
Break my pencils and ask for change
I left my stamina at home
so I need to buy some
Don't want no Fresca
In a hurry to get a rush
No, you can't have first sip
Now I can run in circles
and talk about aliens
A blessed resurgence of
my will to be a member of
the human species
It's like a commercial
so rehearsed
The cycle continues
I go home, slump down
and wait for tomorrow
My life is on rental
75 cents a day

24-7
Thomas B.

The lights grow dim
The drugs kick in
The windows fog up
The door is shut
The beeping has stopped
The camera is off
The cup is cold
The stories are old
The clock has turned
The time has come
My life is done
I go home

Life

Krystle B.

I am thankful
As others mope
I picture a
Photograph in
My head of my
Childhood. During my Childhood
I made Mistakes
And Learned from
Mistakes. Sometimes.
As I look in the Mirror, I look and
Say, Is this Me?
As I look my heart
Is empty, I picture
My Self at a river.
I can fly to a place
Where there is no Hate,
Fear, or Racism. Then I
awaken from this Fantasy
and Realize I'm blessed
With Love and Hope.

Moving Forward
by Jennifer Webster

Blessed with Impossibility,
    My childhood spins
against the tides of night
    to awaken
        broken spirits
    and light a path
        to the beginning.

Untitled
by Jennifer Webster

This morning I smelled patchouli.
    I keep wax in my jewelry box.
It's from a candle I once burned
    for a flame.
It's smell brings me sweetness
    saturates my skin
       and mind,
Every sense becomes one
    and there is just you...

This morning I smelled patchouli;
    it was like a kiss
       of warm moonlight.

She Speaks to Him
by Jennifer Webster

Who are you,
the one in the purple raincoat?
The one who walks the night
while the stars
twinkle on your forehead.
Who are you?
Who tells my brain to open wide,
who shoves your thoughts into the opening,
who *are* you?
Drowning me, stifling my emotions,
smothering my face,
feeling nothing.
Who are you? What do you want?
Why am I so wrong?
Where's my child?
Am I *your* child?
You dropped this egg in my lap
now I have to be careful it doesn't break.
Who are you?
If I could give you back your precious chicks
would you take them?
Would you love them as I have?
Could you? Could I?
Where did you get your power?
I didn't give it to you.
Did you take it from me?
What is my power?
what is my worth?
What is my life?

Hidden deep in the pockets of your purple raincoat,
can I learn to care for myself?
I am nothing; you are everything?

Should I worship you with the mud of my heart on your boots?
Should I give you my body, my spirit, my life?

Will you keep me safe
    underneath your purple raincoat
        where I can never see the stars dance?
    Or will you hold me outside,
        letting rains tear at my mind and body?
    Will you use my power,
        take it for yourself?
    My power,
        robbed by you
            stolen from me.
    I will take back my power
        Control my life.
      Slash through your raincoat
        expose your diminished heart.

I will find my soul
    and fry your brains in my kitchen,
        over my fire.
          Set free my desires.
What mastery will you have over me then?
        You will be nothing.
    Lost in space;
          trapped in a void.
I will be firmly planted in the earth,
    dancing in the air,
        moving with the stars.
I will sing with the moon as you wail in darkness,
        searching for your soul.
No. I won't take your soul.
What need would I have for yours? My own will be enough.
I would not rob you as you have robbed me.
Your misery will be your own;
    stemming from the twisted branches of your existence.
The seeds not planted by me.
        I will be free.
    Worship will not be required.
      You will be free.

To be loving and nurturing,
  caring and forgiving,
    all that is needed.
  Demanding and cold
    I can never be.
Only one and whole, my own self. Happy and beautiful.
I will wear the purple raincoat and walk among the stars.
  I will dance with them.
I will not keep you safely tucked away in my pockets.
  I will give you your own raincoat.
    I will show you the dance.
    But you must learn the steps.

William H. Banks, Jr. is WritersCorps Writer-in-Residence at
Wave Hill and conducts workshops at The Citizens Advice
Bureau. He is the Director of the Harlem Writers' Guild, an instructor
in creative writing at The New School, and co-author of the book,
"Father Behind Bars: The Life of Arthur Hamilton."

I'm a writer because a long time ago someone told me that what I wrote down made sense, and that was not always true of everybody. My professional writing began about 20 years ago. I published a novel, a black college love story, set in the 60s. It got favorable reviews, but at the time books by black authors who were not established usually didn't do well. In 3 or 4 years the book was out of print, and I forgot about writing as a career.

Then one day an acquaintance of mine asked if I'd ever heard of the Harlem Writers Guild. When I thought of the Harlem Writers Guild I thought of John Henry Clark, Maya Angelou. Then I went to some meetings and was really energized. What I saw was that a lot of the same challenges and problems that had beset me as a writer— writing by myself with no encouragement—were shared by this community of African American writers. I would not be writing today were it not for that organization.

The experience of African Americans—like the experience of women or of people who have not had the best of what this society has to offer—is so deep that there is an endless well of stories still to come, that African American writers will never be out of work. Maybe they won't always be paid what they should, but the work will always be there. I'm writing because stories are still untold.

The first thing you have to do with people who want to write, is convince them that what they have to say is important. At the Citizens Advice Bureau we put a vision in front of people. I knew that 1995 was going to be the World War II 50-year commemoration, which was one thing they all had in common. By being blessed to live this long, they have personal stories that nobody else could tell. My presence perhaps showed them a writer with a published book, but each of us had stories, and maybe someone would find their stories valuable at this point in their life.

It was very moving and poignant for me to know people from that era. Their memories are so clear—as though they're from a time capsule. My parents used to tell me about the world before I was born, which was a great source of happiness for me. Working with these seniors was reminiscent of that time.

You don't survive in a world like this—with this much violence, disease and hatred—without having learned some very powerful, profound lessons. Look at the lives of these seniors very closely— they ate right, they worked very hard, they didn't abuse their bodies, they did have families. Sure they have regrets, but they did many things right. Quality is no accident, and neither is long life.

One of the things that gives you a history, a sense of country, of neighborhood, or a person's life, is literary form—to write it down so it can be shared. For WritersCorps to not only exist, but exist in the Bronx is absolutely critical, from the standpoint of developing writing coming out of neighborhoods. That's what makes writing strong, and important to people.

The Bronx has been overlooked artistically, despite the fact that it has, proportionally, as much or more talent as you would find anywhere else—people like Abraham Rodriguez, a fine writer from the South Bronx, or some of our colleagues, many who are Bronx natives, whose work is just as distinguished, just as important. Were it not for programs like WritersCorps to support such talent, it would die. You write and you write, but without recognition, eventually you'll stop.

Writing is important to tell personal stories, to empower people. It fulfills many human ambitions at once and brings you closer to the thought process—whatever that is—in its purest form. Of course, writing is not the first thing that people think of in this world of great desperation and critical need.

One of the great revelations for many young people raised on MTV and CNN is the part the written word plays in TV and film. When they do make that connection—which the schools don't seem to be getting across—it's very empowering. One the things I'd like to do, if we continue, is bring more professionals into the workshops, so the participants see this is real world stuff, that will have meaning after WritersCorps is over.

WritersCorps has been a great opportunity for me to share in the joy and privilege of what writing has meant to me, and it's meant quite a bit. I think I've touched both the lives of the very young and the very old. Those are probably the two most important but, unfortunately, the least regarded segments of this society. I hope WritersCorps continues in those directions.

My First Job in Puerto Rico
by Rosalina P., Morris Senior Center

I believe I was around seventeen years old when I told my mother that I would like to be a nurse. I always talk to my mother first because she was more understanding. I respected my father a lot. But my mother had to tell my father to see if he agreed. He didn't like the idea but my mother insisted.

In those years Puerto Rican people had a family Doctor. So my father talked to our family Doctor and asked him for a favor to train me and not to pay me any salary. The Doctor accepted. I was very excited to start my job, that's what I called it. I learned a lot. The first thing I learned was to learn how to communicate with people. They taught me how to make beds, and how to give a bath to the patients. How to feed them. I had to comb their hair, walk them up and down for exercise, and even make them laugh a little. All this was for free but that was my training.

Meanwhile I applied for a real job in a hospital. When they called me for the interview they did accept me. I really was very happy because I was going to make money. The uniform was not pretty but I didn't mind. I got along with everybody, Doctors, nurses, the pantry girls and mostly with the sick babies. That was the first Ward that I got into.

I was very happy with my Job, but at the same time it was very sad. The crying of the sick babies made me very sad. So later on after a year I talked to my supervisor to change me from that Ward and of course they did. I felt much better working with grown-up people. Even though they were sick they were more understanding and I communicate much better with them. Well, over there I had to work different shifts. Day and nights. It was not very pleasant to be working nights but I had to do it. I had a very good time because I like a job that I move around and make jokes and laugh.

Sometimes we had a very sick person and it was very sad when I came the next morning and I find out that my dear patient had died. But even so I do love the work of the hospitals. When I decided to come to this country that was the type of work that I started to look for. I wish sometimes that I had been a nurse. I love it.

Leaving Home, 1948

by Rosalina P.

I was born in Puerto Rico but I have been in this country since 1948. I remember having the ambition of traveling and being independent. I was 21 years old when I left my family. It was four of us, three girls and one boy. I had good parents but they were very strict. If I wanted to go some place I had to get the OK first not only from my mother but from my father too.

To go shopping my mother had to keep me company. Going to the beach she had to go with us too. Finally I told them that I wanted to come to America. Since I didn't have any relatives over here my father didn't agree but my mother didn't mind. I only had a girlfriend over here. Well I flew to the United states in an army plane, a two motors plane. At the time I didn't know any better.

When we reached this country we had one of the biggest snow storm, that's what I learn later on. The snow was so high that it covered all the cars. I was frightened but I had no other choice but to stay. I was very lucky because I started to work in a week. It was not difficult for me because I learned to speak and write English in Puerto Rico.

Since then I have been here in this country and I love it. Yes I love to go visiting to Puerto Rico, but here I grew in many ways and I learned to be independent in a hard way. I love this country very much.

The End.

The Unwritten Earth

by William H. Banks, Jr.

When William Shakespeare proclaimed: "All the world's a stage," he did not go far enough.

The earth is the stage for the drama and sometime comedy of human history and much more. Earth is the canvas, the tablet, the clay, the stone, the stage and the screen for all human expression. Every modern keystroke and brush stroke, each and every scribble, is recorded on the face of the earth today just as surely as cave drawings were at the dawn of recorded history.

Pages, memory bytes and pixels hold the human story so far. What's left is that portion of nature which has not been touched by human history, and with it's beauty still intact, continues to inspire writers and other artists. What remains in all too few locations is the unwritten earth.

The Bronx Council on the Arts assigned me, a black writer from Harlem to a place that has been described as the Apple's Eden. Wave Hill isn't a neighborhood (no one lives here) but it is a very important community and it is, after all, teaming with life. It's focus is nature and the human connection to it. Wave Hill is one of the city's 21 parks. It is 23 lush acres of land about 18 miles north of the Empire State Building on the banks of the Hudson River. A staff of 30 maintains the site and administers a score of programs which deal with nature study, gardening, ethnobotany, horticulture, landscaping and teacher training.

Surrounded by streams of happy and yet orderly New York City school children on my first day at Wave Hill, I gazed across the Hudson River at the autumn colored cliffs of New Jersey. I remembered something that I must have been told for the first time on an elementary school field trip perhaps forty years ago: The Bronx is the only borough of New York City which is part of the mainland of the United States. I also remembered the value of the summers which I spent in a beautiful and bountiful part of rural Virginia, not in the concrete ovens of the City where sometimes not even hope could grow.

It was then that I could see some things as clearly as the New Jersey cliffs. First, that an urban existence should not and must not preclude a firm connection with nature. Next, I could also see and realize that the natural beauty of America is every citizen's heritage and that part of a writer's job is to capture it and share it with readers.

As writer in residence at Wave Hill, my job is to unearth, as it were, and celebrate the influence of nature on literature. This can be done by exploring the manner in which certain writers place the earth and the environment either in the foreground or in the immediate background of their work. The mission is to strengthen the connection between the earth and literature, through both public programs at Wave Hill and by involvement with an off campus, exploratory program made up of students from Lehman College.

Wave Hill, which celebrates its 30th anniversary in 1995, has a long and well-established tradition as a venue of the performing and fine arts. Hopefully, this new initiative will plant seeds of literary awareness that will flourish at Wave Hill and beyond. Appreciation of nature's role in the literature of yesterday and today is both satisfying and useful. Moreover, awareness of nature's role in the future is critical. The unwritten earth is all we have left.

Paola Corso's stories from her first collection, *"Giovanna's 86 Circles,"* have appeared in various literary magazines. She is co-founder of the National Writers Union New York Local Community Writing Project. As a WritersCorps member, she taught creative writing at Bronx-Lebanon Hospital and gathered oral histories at Mt. Carmel Center for Senior Citizens.

Photo by Wayne Providence

I write to feel complete. I don't feel I have a choice at this point. We moved when I was between 3rd and 4th grade and afterward it took me a long time to make friends. As a result, I spent a great deal of time in my room, writing. I wrote poems and a mystery novel. I could have done any number of things—helped my mother with the Jell-O salad, helped my father cut grass, played with my sister—but I chose to occupy myself with writing and reading, and that experience made me a writer. Writing is my religion. I'm faithful to it, and my reward is self-expression. If nothing else, I've communicated with myself, though there's always the hope that you'll reach others. Self-expression is very empowering. It can cause social and spiritual change, enlightenment. Again, I would equate it with religion. Nobody seems to question the importance of worshipping every week; writing is no different.

Writers have a responsibility to exercise their senses and use them to be visionaries, to see what other people have a harder time seeing, and bring a new dimension to our daily lives—bring a kind of magic to the mundane. In order for change to happen, you have to not only see what is, but envision what could be—as fantasy, magic or dreams.

I have a master's degree in public administration and community organizing and have been a writer for many years, so WritersCorps is a very natural thing for me to do. My expectations of WritersCorps are based on my experience with the National Writers Union. The National Writers Union has the same goal as WritersCorps: working in alternative settings, facilitating creative writing workshops—reaching people who wouldn't otherwise exercise their imaginative skills. Even if the content isn't political, the process of writing and bringing writers into the community is political. At the National Writers Union I learned that setting up workshops was not the easiest thing to orchestrate. So with WritersCorps, I never expected large numbers, but I've come to expect a certain quality.

One of my projects has been working with other WritersCorps members on a play, based on oral history interviews with senior citizens. Hearing individual stories in the course of oral history interviews, or during my creative writing workshops at the hospital, I can't help but get involved on some level with these people's lives. A 93-year-old man I interviewed for an oral history project got very emotional as he recalled memories of people who helped him when he was a homeless boy in Italy. Two weeks later, he died. I've thought about this man ever since. Then one day, I saw a homeless man on the subway, and was very taken by him. I was able to look at this man in a different way. I actually ran into this man again and approached him—perhaps because my recent experience made me more aware of people's vulnerability. This experience has affected my writing as well. I need to be more vulnerable as a writer. That's ultimately what reaches people as readers.

My voice is Italian-American, it's the voice of my grandmother, small town, working class, and I've tried to bring that sensibility to my writing workshops and the readings. Whether or not people have already been exposed to this, I can't know. I do know that Italian-American literature is under represented in the bookstores, so perhaps this might be refreshing in some way.

I've also tried to incorporate my interest in myth, magic and folklore and Italian-American writers into the workshops. In one of my workshops, I showed the class a series of abstract photos, then read some Italian folk tales by Italo Calvino, and had them write their own folk tales. The combination of the magic in the folk tales and the mystery in the photographs led them to write about worlds that they didn't know could exist. Anytime someone makes a discovery like this, they're empowered. The use of magic or make-believe works in some indirect or subconscious way toward social change, self-discovery, and the realization of possibilities. We shouldn't rule anything out. Anything is possible.

Mom
by Betty Morales, Bronx Lebanon Hospital Staff

She fed you
and
only when she was sure that there was
some left after feeding all of you
did she dare take a bite
and
when, about to take a bite,
you screamed for more.
She fed you again.

Grandma
by Willielue Wilkins, Foster Grandparents Program

My earliest memory is of my grandma getting vegetables in her garden. She had turnips and greens growing close to the ground. You had to dig to get the roots up, the soil was so hard, and she didn't keep a fence around it, either.

Grandma was a slave. She was sold two times. First to Mr. Young. Second and last to Mr. Wilkins, my grandfather. She was a full-blooded American Indian with long black braids. Her dress was down to her ankles, and she wore a blue and white checkered apron.

My grandma smoked a handmade corncob pipe. Sometimes she asked me, "Did you see my pipe?" "Yes, Grandma. It's behind your ear." We laughed at that together. We drank coffee together too. Sometimes from the Maxwell House coffee can. It burned my lip.

Grandma's death was the first one for me to know about. I was 6. The day she died, my bigger sister and I were sitting on the porch. She said to me, "Come here. Let me show you something. Look in the mirror." She used a mirror to see what they were doing inside. She held it at just the right angle so we could see them dressing Grandma and combing her hair. I didn't see any gray in her hair. Just black.

My Daddy came on the porch and said to me, "Grandma is gone and she's not coming back. We have to wash her and dress her up and take her to the cemetery. We're going to leave her there now."

When they lowered the casket into the ground, my Dad was holding onto my arm, holding it close to his chest.

The Days After the Dawn
by Barnett Berger, Social Worker, Fulton Psychiatry

For years upon years, the world had been barreling along, not necessarily ignorant of the possible consequences of its high technology tensions but not willing to find balance or compromise amongst its peoples.

One day the inevitable happened, and the explosion was so massive the few survivors who could establish communication with one another called it "the dawn."

And those persons, after realizing that their only hope to survive together in harmony and balance in the days after the dawn were to overcome their grief and depression and build a functional system again, settled upon construction of a 3-level sanctum with each level connected by a simple series of interlocking stairways. And to use these stairways, it was not necessary to announce one's presence or intentions. It was understood that in this sanctum, only the most simple and basic behavior was to be practiced. The lower level of the sanctum housed a fertile garden and the survival colony grew the most basic foods and also created a most simple, rough type of wine out of the vegetables that grew there, that every member of the colony could partake in.

Both the second and the top levels have entrances and exits for people to stroll around the surrounding grounds, but the horizon was limited and there were only hints of things for people to see, so the accesses tended to be made only by families and relatives trying to create a picnic atmosphere or by lovers attempting to rekindle and understand those simple feelings of affection they or their ancestors had once known.

And yet, no matter how hard the colony tried, it was never possible to erase the pain of loss and alienation created by the dawn's void. Even the very architecture of the staircases reminded the people of life lived on different levels on the endless up and down rhythms of a search for balance. For those devoid of companionship or unable to find a specific task the sense of loneliness could be devastating.

Yet nothing ever changed nor could it ever change because the people have now realized in how short a time their world could be brought to a brink.

Better to live with the silence and the absolute routine than to risk the dawn again.

Raw Egg in Beer

(An excerpt from a short story)

by Paola Corso

On the day he was to die, Plum Borough Mayor Salvatore Taviani wore a crisp white shirt. It was bright enough to celebrate the absence of color and starched to ward off temptation from wrinkles. On the brim of his Stetson were wings that took flight on occasion and the diamond on his pinky shone as if it were crowned in a halo. I scribbled in my reporter's notebook that he walked in Fazzio's Tavern at exactly 6:30, the same time he did every other day of the year.

Although the mayor's 86, he's in perfect health, according to his family doctor, who told me Taviani could keep going for another 15 years. He still has rosy cheeks, a gripping handshake, and endurance from swimming every morning. He feeds, bathes and dresses his invalid wife, Elisabetta, every day before working mornings at the borough office and afternoons at the bank he founded. When he has time, he visits development sites where his construction company has been awarded contracts. Then he has a few drinks at the tavern before going home to change into a suit and tie if that evening he has a council meeting.

I was assigned to cover the mayor's last day for the Tarentum newspaper, the Valley Daily News. It was as routine as the daily "Stroller" gossip column for the Valley to print obits celebrating life after someone dies, but plain unheard of to run articles about somebody's death when they were still alive.

The city editor says somehow I've got to get Taviani to talk. What I'd really like to know is how can he be so sure about his fate? Does knowing make a difference? My editor says those kind of questions are fine except that they can't possibly be answered in 10 inches, and that's all the space she's slated for the mayor's story, since a full-page ad from Pittsburgh Plate Glass came in.

"Can't you cut the Stroller?"

"Never have. Never will," she says. She wants a document, a study, a piece of paper that verifies the mayor's alleged claim. A stone tablet would be nice, she says, with or without the burning bush.

After my editor has me write a dozen obituaries of people who we know for a fact are dead, I catch up with the mayor at Fazzio's

94

Tavern. A pair of eyes peers through the blinds like two black notes as I squeeze my car between a navy blue Olds and a dirt-brown Cutlass in the tavern parking lot. I'm a few minutes early so I plop myself down on a bar stool, one of the few empty seats in the house. The bartender doesn't say a word as he walks away from the window.

"Don't give her the evil eye, now. How's she supposed to know?" says a woman as she tugs at the bartender's apron. Lena turns to me and says, "If you sit there, you'll have to buy everybody drinks. That's where the mayor sits."

I leap up from my seat and slide over to face a jar of beef jerky on the counter.

White Christmas lights trim the bar, which is black-stained wood. Gregory, the bartender, says his wife had it varnished that way so fingerprints and dirt wouldn't show. He says he allowed her to do that if she allowed him to keep the Christmas lights up all year round. His wife, Rita, comes out with her hair sprayed stiff and waters the Easter lily on the windowsill. She notices the trumpet flower is facing down, so she sets the sprinkling can on the table and tries to get it to face up, but it goes limp as soon as she lets go.

I pull out my reporter's notebook from my pocket and explain that I'm doing a story on the mayor. I ask questions and wait for someone to slip.

"I hear the doctor says he could live another 20 years. What do you think?"

"Just about anything is possible," Lena says.

Gregory cuts in by recalling the mayor's first job as a paperboy. Instead of walking the route or biking up hills, he bought a motorcycle with a car attached where his brother sat tossing stacks of papers as he drove.

"His parents were immigrants from Calabria. The boot of Italy he calls it. He quit school in the eighth grade, you know, and worked in the coal mines with his father to help support the family," Gregory says. "Course he's practically a millionaire now, but he didn't start out that way."

A man at the bar taps me on the shoulder. "He's shrewd all right. He soaks his friends and fellow businessmen in booze before bidding on a project. That's what he does. He rents a suite and throws a big party. I've been to one of them. Everyone except him drinks."

I keep waiting for someone to so much as acknowledge that

they really think the mayor is going to die today, like he says he is. I can't help but think that either they don't believe him, or they're so faithful to him that they believe everything he says.

It's 6:30. The mayor pauses at the doorway before walking in. He gloats in his good favor. He'll die with a full head of hair—a wish he'd been praying for ever since childhood.

"We've been waiting for you," Lena says.

"Same time, same station everyday," the mayor says.

He sits on the black bar stool, leans against the wall, positioning his shiny black leather shoe on the bar rung right on top of the hole. His other foot dangles. His back is straight as he holds out a glass of beer in one hand while his other forms a loose fist suspended in air, the fingers wiggling as though he's playing a musical instrument.

Within minutes, everyone huddles around him. I expect that they'll confront, once and for all, his death. Instead they talk about food. The menu changes from meatball sandwiches to veal cutlet.

"That settles it. No skimping—veal parmesan, a side plate of pasta, salad, garlic bread and two vegetables." I'm convinced they're talking about his wake, then I hear the mayor add, "The only ground rule is that you stay out of the kitchen while I cook."

A sign behind the bar flashes, "Raw egg with beer."

"Get ready. It's cock-a-doodle-doo time," Lena announces.

Gregory reaches into the refrigerator and hands a basket to the mayor. When the Christmas lights flash on, it's as though a mountain of eggs magically appears. Each alternates between shining like marble and returning to a dim shell with its unfinished flatness. Everyone jumps off their stools to form a line as they take turns getting an egg from the mayor. He hands one to all patrons in the bar except me because I stay put in my seat. Somehow, everyone keeps pace with the cadence of the lights. They return to their places one by one and wait for the mayor to take the last egg in the basket and crack it on the rim of his glass. When they hear the fragile sound, it's as though a bell goes off. They all crack their egg in a mug of beer and turn to face him. The mayor raises his glass high above his head and gazes at it the way a priest does a chalice before he drinks the blood of Christ. Everyone raises their glass in the air at the same time.

"Cock-a-doodle-doo," the mayor says.

"Cock-a-doodle-doo," they all say, repeating the mayor's words and intonation before chugging the egg and beer concoction down.

An all-out procession follows. The mayor leaps off his stool and begins flapping his arms and waddling his rear end and turning his feet out. He waddles from checker to checker on the floor all the way to the window. His feathery moves almost turn into a slow-motion disco dance with the help of the flashing lights. He settles back into his warm seat. Everyone follows as if the mayor were doing some prescribed step like the polka or the fox trot or the tango.

"Why the raw egg?" I ask Gregory.

"The mayor's papa was a coal miner. And the story goes that when he crawled out of that big black hole in the earth at the end of the day, his lungs were so full of coal dust, there was no room left for air. He rested his hand on his chest and wheezed and snorted and gasped just to push and pull every breath he'd take. He might as well've been playing the accordion. When the Mrs. heard the old man coughing outside the door, she greeted him by handing him a hose to wash off in the courtyard where the hens wandered from the coop after laying eggs. One day, a stray hen squatted and laid an egg right smack in the middle of a steaming puddle of soot. The egg was as white as that puddle was black. He couldn't believe that a hen would lay an egg on a bed of wet coal dust and took it for a miracle. His papa slipped the egg in his pocket and sat at the supper table. Grime was still caked under his fingernails even after a good scrubbing to clean it out, which made the Mrs. upset when she saw his 10 stubby mine shafts grabbing for a white napkin.

"His papa said, 'That dirt is deeper than the coal. I can't get that out.'

"'You dig out the coal, every last ounce of it, don't ya?' she said.

"'That's cause we're buried alive down there for Christ's sake,' he said, cracking the egg in his pocket as he shifted in his seat.

"'Not if you were the mailman,' she said. She had always wanted him to work in a clean office and handle white envelopes.

"'You don't want me licking stamps all day getting dry in the mouth. Least I can come home and kiss ya,' he told his wife.

"Normally after dinner, he'd drop off on the couch with the newspaper on his chest, but that day he pulled out the egg and finished cracking it in a glass of beer and swallowed it. He felt the yolk slide down his throat and land in his stomach. Not long after that, feathers started growing inside. He knew because they tickled him so much he squirmed until he fell off the couch and started to roll on the floor and scratch his belly. The Mrs. grabbed a broom and started beating him with it because she thought he had some kind of varmint crawling inside his gutchies. The mayor says that's when his papa got up and did a jig around the room with the Mrs. hanging over his shoulder like a sack of potatoes. All of a sudden, he had so much life in him, he flew to the roof and crooned at the top of his lungs one long note that seemed to last forever and ever, to make up for all the air sucked out of him little by little with every short, inner tube gasp and crankshaft cough and pickled snort and karate chop hack and whistling wheeze from working in a coal mine all those years of his life. He got his breath back."

D on **Gellver De Currea-Lugo** was born in Santafé de Bogotá, Colombia. He has acted, written, directed and produced theater, film, video and television, and was awarded the Focine Award for Best Actor, and Columbia's ACJ-YMCA for Best Director. His scripts have placed in competitions in Cuba and Spain, and his play, "Sleeping Bag" was published in the *"Ollantay Theater Magazine"* in New York. For WritersCorps he worked at Hostos Community College.

Photo by Mafe Rueda

It's an accident that I am a writer, and that accident had many causes. I first wanted to be an architect. Next I studied psychology, philosophy, theology and theater. I took up philosophy and theater at the same time, studying philosophy all day and theater at night, until I became ill. My psychiatrist told me I must choose between the two, so I chose the theater. I applied for a fellowship to study film in Russia, but I didn't have the money for the ticket. In the meantime, I had written many poems and got the idea to make a book and sell it and make money. Those poems weren't very good, however and fortunately, weren't published.

It happened that I was cast in a movie, and while I was on the road, the sound track lady asked me if I had anything to read, because she was bored. All I had was my poems. Well, she wasn't interested in the poems but said, if I could write a 30-minute script she would be interested.

I started writing a screenplay but didn't know what to write about. So I watched many movies and learned the culture of films, and how they tell stories. I wrote my screenplay about a young writer who had to write a screenplay at the request of a lady producer!

After I finished the script, I got the leading role in a film, "VISA USA." I showed the Cuban producers my script and they thought it was fabulous, and suggested I send it to the Havana Film Festival. I did, and won the third prize! Meanwhile, in Colombia they considered me a very frivolous person—a "show business" type and didn't take me seriously, because my style—my way of looking at the world—is so different, it's unacceptable there, and because I am very crazy anyway. So when the Cuban filmmakers liked my work, I was astonished—that someone who knew film was telling me how good it was—and also that the first people to recognize my work were foreigners!

I wrote a lot for TV — promotions, commercials, soap operas and a TV series. The TV series was called "El Gallinazo," and wasn't very successful, because I had to make too many concessions to satisfy the commercial aspect of the business. From then on, I wrote only for myself. I found writing an indescribable pleasure—to amuse myself by inventing and transforming the world around me.

One of my friends told me that if I can make progress with my work in Colombia—where they don't encourage or support artistic

(Editor's note: This is based on an interview translated by Juan Goméz Quiróz)

lifestyles—I would do even better in another part of the world. I don't know why, but I've always wanted to live in New York, not Paris, London or Moscow, not Hollywood, but New York. It's such a challenge to learn English, but I came to this life to learn. That is my mission. It has nothing to do with religion or mysticism. New York has taught me a lot in a very short period of time.

WritersCorps has provided a backdrop for me. More than that, I have had the opportunity of being my own teacher. When I came here I didn't know anyone—I didn't know the culture, the customs. I come from a tropical country, so this is another world. Here you have to learn how the city moves, or you're out of step. All this I must teach myself.

With WritersCorps, I'm working with the Hostos College Pepatian Dance Company. The project is very interesting. They have selected ten families from the South Bronx, and we are writing a play based on the history and experience of those families in New York. Out of their stories we're creating a performance. This is a multimedia performance which includes video, film, dance, and theater. I'm learning a lot. It's a very emotional experience for me to be involved in creating something with all these elements that I'm not familiar with.

I think WritersCorps should take more chances and be less academic—just as I have taken chances in my own work, or as others have. Without risk there wouldn't be this anthology, I wouldn't have collaborated in this work at Hostos. Artists are not just *homosapiens*, those who think; artists are those who make things, *homofabrique*—the dreamers. When one is a creator, you have to keep searching for creative possibilities, not because it's a duty, but for the risk, the pleasure, the adventure of being alive.

The world doesn't only need writers, it needs people who read. It also needs an audience—people who like to enjoy themselves. I like to see life as a joke—a game. And in this game, if nothing is taken seriously, then we must look for the best way to enjoy ourselves, because life knows more than we do. My first book of poems is called "Someone Near You Has Just Finished Not Committing Suicide," because, in a way, I already died once. I hit bottom on every level—personally, artistically, emotionally, psychologically. In Colombia, death is not a poem; it's not the news; it's an everyday reality.

I don't know why literature was invented, but to me it's a

medium that I can use to tell my stories. There is always a story to tell. There are many stories, many cultures, many situations, many styles—enough to get everybody confused—but it's a divine confusion. Just as when I read Haiku from Japan, and the beauty and perfection with which it captures the essence confounds me, it then becomes a challenge, and I'll try to confuse them back. You have to be one step ahead.

Familias

Editor's note: The following is a description of the "Familias" multi-media project to be performed December 1995 at Hostos Community College with Pepatian Dance Company, excerpted from Don Gellver's WritersCorps Final Report. Translated by Paloma Monje.

The Hostos Center for the Arts and Culture, part of Hostos Community College, today is a stabilizing element in the South Bronx. It's also the only College in the City University of New York that attends to the Hispanic Communities' need with bilingual programs. It has become one of the preeminent centers for multi-art presentations for New York's Latino community.

Since 1983 Pepatian Dance Company has created popular, critically-acclaimed projects integrating dance, music, literature, film and video to explore and comment on urban Latino reality, mythology and popular culture.

"Familias" is a multi-disciplinary theatrical production emerging directly from a process of intensive interpersonal research, exploring the place and natural setting of a family in an urban community, through the experience of several generations of immigrant families living in New York's South. Bronx neighborhood. *"Familias"* will be created by choreographer Merián Soto and visual artist Pepón Osorio, in collaboration with composer Carl Royce, filmmaker Irene Sosa, and a company of eight performers with ten local families.

This project, which began in April 1994, will continue through November 1995, when the world première of *"Familias"* will take place in six consecutive performances at the Hostos Center.

The original proposal of the Pepatian Company was to incorporate every member of the project into a collaborative entity, so that in different ways a personal bond could be established in order to capture the cultural environment—the customs and the individual behavior—of all the participants within the dynamics of coming together. The members were given much liberty for research, but always respectful of the privacy of the home shared. We were careful not to become emotionally involved in each other's personal lives.

Within the families are Chilean political activists, once tortured and persecuted by the Pinochet regime of the 1970s. They currently function in a cultural and communal center called "La Peña del Bronx." Members of another *familia* are also related to "illegal" activity, like the Mexicans who sell candy on the No. 4 subway line in New York, who are frequently caught and incarcerated. Other *familias* include a Honduran DJ; a Dominican cultural activist who is a single parent of a teenage girl, and lives in a constant struggle with the growing needs of her child. There is also a Puerto Rican-Cuban woman who works with family social programs. She was the victim of an alcoholic father and domestic violence. Another *familia* consists of a homosexual man raising his adopted child. His work informs the Latino community about the dangers of unsafe sex. Finally, other *familias* are former and current welfare recipients. The most overwhelming social determinant of the *familias* is the absence of the father as a family role model.

Another objective of the project was to develop a camaraderie with "La Peña del Bronx" in which all of Pepatian Dance Company members and the participating *familias* introduced each other at a party to share our experiences. A month later an altar was conceived by the group for the purpose of involving the *familias* in a process of communal sharing. The altar was stored at an individual's house, and every month it was taken to another house. I wrote the following poem which was part of the altar:

> We
> who are being born—
> joy
> hope
> and
> pain
>
>
> We—
> different roads
> unknown
> who grow with life
> make mistakes
> learn
> forget
> and
> teach
>
>
> We
> ask forgiveness

and
are thankful for
all the days
of having united
in love's smile

What I find lacking in terms of the overall approach of the WritersCorps, in regards to this project in the South Bronx, is the absence of conceptualizing in-depth areas related to anthropological and sociological investigation worthy of this community's history. The rich cultural heritage of this community is impossible to generalize in simple terms. This program could be even more effective if the contribution that the community makes was acknowledged and valued, rather then simply being the focus of our teaching. In other words, we should not just pretend to be the teacher to these *familias*, we should learn to become their students.

Someone Near You
Just Finished Not Committing Suicide

(selected poems) by Don Gellver

OF THE THEORIES WITHOUT PRAXIS

EVOLUTION THEORY

the bird aims
without tenderness

A stone
blossoms in the eye
of the slingshot

translated by
Silvio Martinez Palau

106

Don Gellver
AESTHETIC THEORY

the rope
the tree
and the lack of creativity
of the one hanged

To William Gil
In Memoriam and
Ad Honorem

translated by
Don Gellver

Don Gellver
HAPPINESS THEORY

From the leaky hose
a few drops
escape to freedom

translated by
Miguel Falquez-Certain

ALTERNATIVE THEORY

To fade
the rainbow
to color
the spring

KNOWLEDGE THEORY

The suicidal
in contrast
to Judas' kiss
: totally given
without treason

translated by
Nancy Davila

Don Gellver

OF THE FUTURE

VIRGINITY AND POLITICS

Repressed
on the tip of a match
the tear of light
discovers fire
while experimenting
with freedom

translated by
Silvio Martinez Palau

LIFE CYCLE

One's born
-not on
judgment day-
grows
-dying all the while-
perhaps one will reproduce
and surely die

Unforeseen events
are rarely mentioned
because
at times
One also
falls in love

To: Victor
the brother that admires
me the most

translated by
Silvio Martinez Palau

OF THE PRESENT

WOMAN

At the very last minute
I realized
God had
one extra rib

To: ERNESTINA LUGO DE CURREA

translated by
Silvio Martinez Palau

UNVIOLATED CORRESPONDENCE
OR THE NEIGHBOR'S WOMAN

Like
in an envelope
without stamps
or addressee
all
alone
She
is inside her sheets

translated by
Miguel Falquez-Certain

EPITAPH

Not only
from humor
did I survive

Chance
was the oracle
in this battle
that life
won
my life

translated by
Miguel Falquez-Certain

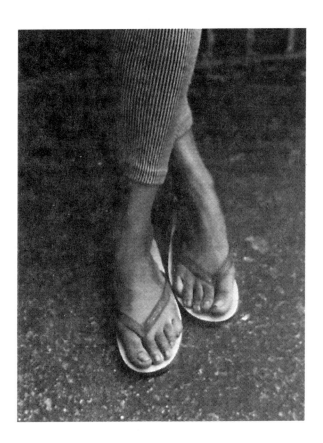

j ennifer jazz began as a percussionist and vocalist in various noise and improvise bands in the East Village underground in the 1980s. She has explored performance, painting, dance and literature in solo and collaborative works in Europe and New York. She is the recipient of the Barbara Deming Memorial Fund for Feminist Fiction, and funding from the Bronx Council on the Arts toward publication of her photo diary, *"bronx brazil."*

Photo by Blair Martin

There are a lot of layers to why I'm a writer. In one sense I made a logical decision that writing was what I wanted to do, but then in a subliminal way I'm a writer because I'm afraid of dying and it's an attempt to leave things in my absence.

I've worked with a lot of different media, but writing is distinct, there's a lot of power in it. The serious ways in which we transmit information to each other are done through writing, and I wanted to be part of a dominant media. In a prankish way—to be in a library with a voice like mine—I wanted to penetrate what I considered closed. William Burroughs says language is a virus. I wanted to let loose a bug in literature.

My introduction to writing was through curriculum at school. I was doing the reading I had to do, but was also doing illicit reading: Iceberg Slim, Donald Goinés. . . comic books—that was *the word.* You didn't get the green light to do that. The only thing that blew me away in school—that changed my life—was *"Metamorphosis"* by Franz Kafka.

A lot of writers have only been read as curriculum writers to the point where they don't have any power at all, because entire school systems have sucked them up to being the representatives of literature and they're discussed in a standardized way. That did not help me. A lot of my writing was not inspired by writing, but by really bad television and movies, and music.

What's interesting about this program is that they have recruited writers in the field who have been experimenting, who have been published, who have their own idiosyncratic approaches to writing. I think that's the only saving grace—the struggle to create an environment to do that. On the one hand you feel this program supports that, and on the other hand there seems to be no regard for what you may need personally. In the future they might train people to teach writing, send them out, and they won't have to be writers.

What I bring to my students is experience on the street, hands-on, teach-yourself experience that's not academic. My kids really respond to that, and all the discussions that come out of that about not needing permission. I definitely am there to tell my kids, look, you can do it, you don't need permission, you just have to want to do it. I'm a living example of that. No one gave me permission, yet I'm here, I'm functioning.

People always ask me, "What writing program do you come out of?"—I don't! In a sense I'm proud of that. In another sense, I'm quite interested now in studying because I'd be sure what I need, as opposed to people who come out of writing programs who have no voices, who are just good.

There's the whole notion of "Who should be writing?" I think in college it opens up, but in elementary school and junior high and high school most of the writers you'll read will probably be from a similar background, describing similar cultural experiences. I think discussions about multiculturalism are very condescending because it's not an issue of multiculturalism, like were being generous. It's really a matter of describing what's happening. New York is a very heterogeneous city.

A lot of the kids—because the curriculum is so far removed from their reality—will make the assumption that they should not write because writing is not about people like them. It's a logical assumption to make. I made it. I thought, wow, all of these books by black women all seem to allude to the South and slavery; they all seem to be very puritanical, so I better not talk about sex or say that I'm enjoying it. I was nervous to do what I did. So in terms of what I bring to my classroom, it's all of that enthusiasm of just going for it, and I think a bit of success with it too. In one of my classes I know my kids are real happy I'm there.

A lot of what I'm writing is not for children to read. To do this thing, I have to think with two heads. I have to say, "I'm a artist," and I go into the schools the same way a Peace Corps volunteer goes into the bush—it's pure charity. The stipend is a token gesture from the government. I accept it, but it's not really a job, because obviously I'm not making enough to live on; I'm spreading what I know out of the kindness of my heart. I spend a lot of time thinking about my kids and I'm not getting paid to do that.

My kids don't have a contemporary sensibility. That really is a big issue with a writer like me, who is very post modernist and doing camp-like stuff. I need an audience that can pick that up. My kids at best are being taught to read and write, and if they're attempting to read literature they're reading literature that is very old.

To teach kids poetry they have to understand abstraction. To teach them abstraction they have to understand all the impulses historically that have led us to the point where we cannot express ourselves the same way that people once did. We need many people to come out and make this possible.

For AmeriCorps to consider this project something they can be really proud of they need to understand that there is this big gap between the rate at which new information is happening and the rate at which it's being transmitted to the mainstream. Kids are coming through these warehouses of old information and all this new shit is happening, so by the time they graduate they're out of it. Their education has gotten in the way of them learning because they've been removed from processes that are much more stimulating.

I think AmeriCorps should re-approach this in terms of not just going into bad neighborhoods to scatter help, bread, cheese or teachers to talk about writing for 2 years. What they really should do is ask, how can we uplift this country and change this country so people are really thinking and we're moving away from metaphors of war.

We're talking about moving into the next millennium as a peace-loving, artistic, creative society that can survive, that has ecological wisdom. If we really do consider ourselves the main force in the universe, as Americans certainly do, we've got to really educate people.

I don't think there is any commitment in this country to art or literature—or literacy—beyond its function in terms of people as consumers. So I'm very cautious when art is discussed by the government, in what capacity it's being discussed. People still think art is this fringe thing that should be scattered to the kids as recreation, when, in actuality, art is just another language that we use. When you discuss the world, you can discuss it atomically, through physics, or aesthetically, in terms of the senses through art, but it's the same reality. Art is no less important than anything else. Art is not a hobby. It needs to be addressed very, very seriously.

from PS122

"song of the water lilies"
by Jose P.

sing a song of colors
of soft petals in sunlight
sing a muted lilies song music blooms
in the still water

"buddies"
by Jose P.

a boy & girl can be buddies
not the kind who run in sunshine
together
or gather for games of sport but buddies
of another sort
who meet just at mealtimes
maybe and
trust.

"the tree"
by Jose P.

it graces our yard
bears beautiful fruit. we breathe deeply the sight of it. the
scent we touch it gently.

"spud-the-crud"
by Pedro P.

spud-the-crud escaped from jail and luis the police
officer was very stupid but his boss sent him because
he was new in the group.
spud was very strong. he was a fighter of stronger men.
when luis went to try to get spud, the other police
officers were laughing at luis because he couldn't get
spud. when the police officers were laughing, luis found
spud and he got him. he brought spud to the jail and the
police officers stopped laughing because the boss named
luis the best policeman of the month.

"my kitchen"
by Luz M.

my kitchen is beautiful. i like it there because there we cook things. my kitchen is small. but i like it. the window has curtains, yellow with different flowers, and when i want to enter the kitchen, it always smells like food because always someone is cooking. i see my kitchen like a camp with a lot of flowers that smell beautiful. i hear animals like dogs, cats, and birds, and i love the sound of the birds. i feel that when i'm in the kitchen, i'm in a new world that nobody is in, only me. the birds, the animals, that world is only my world that i create. i love it. it's beautiful. and in my kitchen is a television. sometimes i do my homework in the kitchen because there's no place better to do homework than my kitchen.

"larry locus and the demons"
(excerpt)
by Angel G.

once, there was a man named larry locus. it was the beginning of the 21st century. he lived in this beautiful house in west virginia. he had a beautiful wife and two sons. one day this telegram came for larry. the telegram said: "larry, you need to go to jupiter right away!" larry always kept a laser gun in a secret compartment so he took the gun. he had a spaceship in a secret room. larry took his gun and a sword and went into the ship. the ship blasted off into space. larry was 2,000 miles from planet earth. he weighed 175 pounds. there was a station for refueling for space crafts. larry refueled and landed on jupiter. when he landed, he weighed 233 pounds. larry was ready for anything. he had to sleep outside in the stars. he needed a suit and a mask to protect himself from the cold and gases. about midnight he heard a noise. when he opened his eyes, he saw a demon. the demon asked "what are you doing here?" "I'm on a mission to capture evil demons," larry told him.

"my special mother"
by Julie F.

my mother is good. i say that because she sometimes lets me see television or skate in the hallway. she tells me to do my homework, reads me stories, she brings me food. the food she brings me is broccoli, rice and beans mixed, and turkey. the nickname that she calls me is "chula" or sometimes "morena!"

"cool mom"
by Bryan P.

my mother is cool because she plays video games. i think she is the only mom that does this. she cooks the best too — everything except broccoli. she likes to buy me clothes. sometimes she screams at me but that doesn't matter. i deserve it.

excerpts from " *bronx brazil*"
(a foreign movie)

by jennifer jazz

Nena

The men in my bodega are so charismatic. The way they shake
open a bag with a quixotic shake of the wrist and
count money with their fingers poised to show off their
gold bracelets and rings. Jose's hair is impeccably
styled, each strand jet black and combed into place with
a vain hand. His mustache is clipped just right and his
belly hangs over the belt of his pants as a sign he is
eating well, and drinking well even in America. Rubio
drinks strong coffee and eats ham on white bread each
morning without a worry, making me wonder if the key to
good health is not what you eat but how you eat it.
Ismael is always saying that there are no more esposas
in Santo Domingo because they're all here! tudo bem.
everything's fine.
I guess their heads are full of the same conflicts as mine
but they have a special gift to deal with it all, because everyday I
go to the bodega needing not just groceries
and the daily newspaper but that atmosphere of warmth,
humor and compassion that I can't find anywhere else
and when I'm short, Jose says "o.k. Nena" with an
omnipotent shrug, as if nothing can stop his profits, as if
no matter what, everything will add up in the end the way
it's supposed to.

art pills

by jennifer jazz

this block
has been crossed by so many feet for so many
reasons, it has meaning invested in it constantly.

it belongs to whoever it touches bekus grayness is
unpossess-able bekus a city is blown up from specks
grain accumulating into more grain
a constancy that never affects you
everywhere
complex
dancing points
that vomit gristle
frantic swarming
nowhere pores grain
inlays of chaos circles utopias

scars & art are pimples

dissolving lines between public & private

by jennifer jazz

there used to be a gang of crackheads that camped out
in the park who spent a lot of time wandering back and
forth from the park to white plains road to cop, then back
to the park again to smoke. i don't see them anymore so i
can only assume that they're dead or in jail because if
they weren't being sussed by the cops they were being
cursed by the shopkeepers they stole from, or getting
into hysterical disputes with the dealers about money
they owed and a lot of times the dealers wouldn't serve
them—even when they'd beg—i once saw a dealer
beat one of them up, which strikes me as penny foolish
as well as sadistic, but the dealers strangely enough,
seemed to despise them.
crackheads are always about to score or on their way
from scoring, this kind of fervor about medication is
fascinating to me. as two of them were passing me by
one night, i overheard one remark to the other that
getting the results to a blood test was the most self-
illuminating experience she'd ever had. . . arguing with
each other day in and day out. . . playing at friendships
that held up as long as there were drugs. . . all of them but
one have disappeared. he must be almost 7 feet tall,
wears glasses and is kind of handsome. i see him
sometimes still pushing a shopping cart through the
streets as if he's touring the aisles to a cosmic
department store and one day when i was rushing by
him under the 'el,' we actually made eye

contact the way men and women do and i
was scared after that that i'd lost what little
distance from the seedy element
in the neighborhood i have, that
i'd really made a mistake in
letting a crackhead appreciate me
as a woman, but the next time i

saw him he was
picking through my
garbage and he looked up
at me with a blank
expression that was not an echo
of the last look and i hurried by,
pretending i didn't see him and
this was how, i suppose, he
won back the
privacy that he needed
to pick through
my garbage and i won back the
glory i needed
to let him.

I LIKE TO DANCE IN TIME BUT BEATS
CONSPIRE
WITH BLOWS WHERE POETRY IS ABSENT. my

favorite lens is blue like when i'm sitting in

front of the t.v. watching

SONIA BRAGA or Deneuve and scribbling in my

notebook the future will be pointy/all

angles and lines as essential as blades. IF I

want a jungle I'll just say "jun-gle" Write

LOvenotes on MS Dos WOrd for windows OR play

sambas on a button AND call

it

perfume.

by jennifer jazz

the politics of place
by jennifer jazz

i've been trying to include myself in the world for as long
as i remember, yet i still remain mostly a spectator. even
when i look at pictures taken from my photo albums, i'm
only observing myself being an observer. maybe i'm a
part of a whole that can't be divided. maybe i'm dead
and any old souvenir will do.
i've been in the northeast bronx for 8 years, after having
spent very intense periods of my life in other parts of
new york and europe. when i first found out i was
pregnant, i had this knee jerk feeling i should leave and
find a more suitable place to have a baby, so i went
down to harlem for a few months, then found myself
back in the bronx. the north bronx is the place i chose to
settle down and raise my son, i think, because the
buildings are all beige or faded pink and the sidewalk is the same
color as the sky and nothing has happened
here yet so my son, in a sense, is being born in a place
that is being born with him. if i stand in front of my house
on a clear day and face west, i'm mesmerized by the
crosses between the pines of woodlawn cemetery. if i
walk closer, and it's past three in the afternoon, i hear the ecstatic
cries of the reincarnated running wild in the
playgrounds that surround it. if someone were to ask me
if the cup is half-empty or half-full, i would say "both!"
my son and i spend a lot of time on the train, traveling
here and there and how weird it is visiting sections of

manhattan where the only other black women are
nannies taking care of white children and where many of
the white mothers, after years of being deceived by a
supremacist fantasy, cringe away from me and my child
in confusion. they say ignorance is bliss, but these
mothers are haunted by reality, which seems sad to me.
their need to control and separate their space from mine,
makes them the exact opposite of mothers in my
neighborhood, who are mostly single, broke,
and pretty damned accepting about whatever happens

as long as it doesn't cost too much, which is why i like it
around here. it's not an up and coming enclave in the
middle of someone's else's ghetto. nobody can lay claim
to it because the original inhabitants died a long time
ago and or left voluntarily and the ones that stayed are a
breed of common sense people that don't let the
constant transition of faces, languages, or occasional
guns popping in the night, scare them away from
attending mass at st. mary's on sunday or stop them
from lining up for quarter rolls and fresh bustelo at
ismael's bodega afterwards.

when you're talking about the world, you're talking about
possibilities, not one fixed, unchangeable idea. if it
sounds like i'm promiscuous, i'm certainly that and worse
because when i see a graffiti on the sides of buildings, i
see a diary and when garbage is strewn all over the
ground on monday morning, i see the aftermath of a
carnival, streamers, confetti, and the bones of a feast,
and when the 2 train bursts out of the tunnel from
manhattan, i remember gray is my favorite color
because gray is the resolution of polarities, the unifying
head between solos that exiles the devil AND jesus, until
the only difference between uptown and downtown is
time.

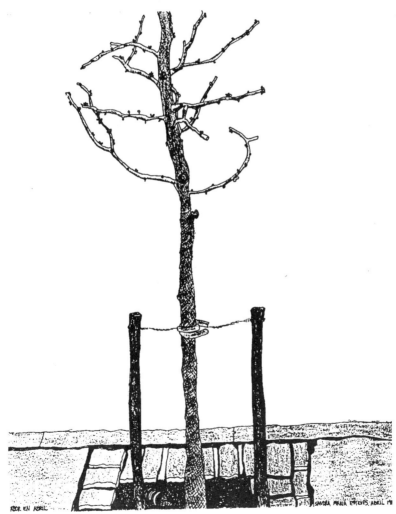

by Sandra María Esteves

alone

alone all alone nobody
but nobody can make it
out alone. if you listen
close I'll tell you what
I know. rain killed my
cat.

I don't know why
my friend died now
I'm home alone but nobody
but nobody can make
it out of here.

Love every body
peace.

Jvonne W., C.E.S. 90

130

2.

Sandra María Esteves
Howard Simon
Jesús Papoleto Meléndez
Juan Gómez Quiróz
Ana Ramos
Karen Green
Majora Carter
Mary Hebert
Wayne Providence

Sandra María Esteves, born and raised in the Bronx, is the author of 3 volumes of poetry. Her work has appeared in over 55 anthologies, magazines and literary journals, most recently *"Unsettling America"* and *"Aloud, Voices from the Nuyorican Poets Cafe."* She was WritersCorps poet-in-residence at the Bronx Museum of the Arts where she conducted poetry workshops.

Photo by Wayne Providence

Writing for me is an art form. From the time I was seven, I wanted to be an artist. I was an extremely withdrawn child, and I suspect that there was abuse in my history. I definitely come from a dysfunctional family, so when I was five my mother sent me to a Catholic boarding school. I guess the trauma of being separated from my family and being among strangers made me withdraw, retreat into my inner light. I would sit for hours drawing and not talk. One reason I didn't talk was because I was told immediately that I couldn't speak Spanish, and under the threat of a plastic tennis racket was forced to speak English. By the time I was in third grade, I knew English and Spanish, but there was some confusion as to what words went to what language. The perfect resolution was not to talk, but draw. I basically didn't talk until I was thirteen.

Even though I didn't like English, I won awards for writing. But I wanted to be an artist, and studied fine and media arts in college. One day, in sculpture class, my instructor displayed sheets of typing paper on the wall that described sculptures you couldn't fabricate physically, only mentally, and I realized that words were another way to create images and pictures. I began to experiment with language and ideas: instead of color, form and line, there were sound, concepts and time.

When I began writing, I met Papoleto and read some of my poetry to him. He said, "I like what you're doing, you should read with me," and immediately I began reading my work publicly. I was terrified. It was so difficult that sometimes I wouldn't show up. I was also embarassed because I didn't consider myself a poet. To me, a poet was someone who had mastered literature and language and was versed in the classics. At that time, I was the only Puerto Rican woman reading in a sea of male poets. The men had books out and very much influenced my work. Along the way I discovered my own issues. Nobody was talking about birth or women's issues, which were important to me, and these subjects began surfacing in my work.

Writing, for me, means transformation. I transform from this reclusive, extremely introverted individual through writing, and through my interactions with other writers. I met all the writers in the New York scene when I started out. Each one became a teacher; each one gave me new insight. I didn't study writing at the university—my university was hanging with these writers. We would meet three or four times a week to try out stuff, listening and talking to each other—fighting about it. That's how my transformation came about—discovering myself in the world, not only as an individual, but in a social-cultural context, and that was important to me as a Latina. We can only go so far on our own, and to go farther, we need someone to pull us out of our shells—we need the light of another. That's how we empower each other, how we teach each other.

We need writers to learn how to communicate in non-violent ways. We already know how to communicate violently—we know that very well. Writing can be violent and threatening, but we don't have to kill anyone to get to the other side of what we're trying to say. We need ideals. Many people don't have communication skills and are unable to express the turmoil that they feel. Writers, whether we intend to or not, become advocates for whole groups—each writer represents at least a hundred thousand people or more. Writers give voice to issues.

What I do in WritersCorps I do anyway, and have been doing since 1973, when I met Papo. We immediately formed a group and were the cultural wing of the Puerto Rican Socialist Party at the time. Whenever the Party had a political activity, they would bring the poets and musicians to unite folks and stir up people's thinking. There were struggles, even then, about our purpose, about how to interact with the community.

When I was growing up there were no literary models around, even though the Puerto Rican community has a rich and extensive literary history. So one thing we're doing, with the help of WritersCorps, is empowering our communities with knowledge of our cultural inheritance, making our community aware of our literature. We have a path and a history that's been deliberately taken away from us. Part of the colonial plan was to keep the masses ignorant. Maybe if people had a sense of self-worth, they wouldn't turn to drugs so easily.

My mission is to cultivate a dialogue, which can take many different forms: a newspaper, a poetry reading, or writing workshop to get people in touch with their inner voice in a non-threatening way. When I first went into my site at the Museum, I was surprised at how violent the kids were to each other in the presence of another teacher, who was humored by some of their abusive behavior. I had to get the kids to be receptive, to listen to other voices, to look at literature and allow it to transform them. I had to get them to be still so they could listen to their inner voices, and to each other.

I think WritersCorps could be a model for communities. Our educational system is in crisis, and I'm very concerned, because I have children in the school system and I'm obligated by law to put my children in a very dangerous environment everyday. Not only is the environment dangerous because of the drugs, artillery, and the racism—which is something that's not even talked about—they're not getting the education they are supposed to. Not only have art and music been eliminated from the regular school program, but our kids are going to school to suffer and be deprived, instead of being enriched. Perhaps WritersCorps can provide a model for education to take place in the community instead of schools. We're talking about education beyond a structured syllabus: How do we encourage people to think for themselves, to come up with creative solutions to the problems we live with? That's what art does: art stimulates the creative part of us so we can find solutions. If there aren't any to be found, we'll dream them up.

My Tree

by Lucinda, Jovonne, Alia, Yaasmiyn, Elizabeth, Shinair,
Cheyenne, Joy, Raquelin, and Sandra María Esteves
—The Bronx Muses

My tree is an adventurous place
to go hide out and play

My tree grows wonderful jewelry
gold jewelry with no silver

My tree is the kind of tree that grows money
That's why I love it
It also made me a millionaire. I wish.

My tree is when I can see beautiful things
from tree to tree

My tree is a spider. It wraps up flies.
It sucks the blood of flies.
But it could talk. I talk to it.
I teach it to talk. I love my tree.

My tree is a place where I run to when I cry.
It is my runaway. I always write, think, see in my tree.
My tree is me. It is my love tree.

My tree is a home
for ten thousand birds.
Each one singing it's own love song.

My tree is a place
to contain the beating wings
of my thoughts.

My tree is my imaginary world which I rule
and which is a forest full of all animals.

My tree is the tree of life
From roots to fruits.

The Mother of Hercules
by Roosevelt H.

I think he should protect us from getting into trouble. I think God is a girl. I think God makes water by crying. I think snow is sugar flakes that he pours from his backyard. I think that he is our Mother. I think God is careful with his clothes. I think God has children. I think her kids are like Hercules. I think she is that.

Untitled
by Lucinda E.

To be nice
and sweet
you have
to change
your attitude
you have to change
your self no one
can change you
only you can change
your self

Spagetti
by David A.

S-Spaghetti is good for eating
P-Parmesan cheese is what I put on it
A-Anything is good but Spaghetti is the best
G-Good, Good, Good, Great
E-extra cheese is the best
T-Try to eat spaghetti with a spoon
T-Terrible rotten spaghetti
I-Impossible to eat

The Unthought
by Tyron H.

The Dog was Shot, Squashed,
Smashed, Tore Apart, Blown up and
SWEPT AWAY.

alone
by Jvonne W

alone all alone nobody
but nobody can make it
out alone. if you listen
close I'll tell you what
I know. rain killed my
cat. I don't know why
my friend died now
I'm home alone but nobody
but nobody can make
it out of here.

Love every body,
peace.

A Job

by Sandra María Esteves

A job means
More than a paycheck
Finding a place in the world
Working for your own thing
Telling your caseworker to kiss your a..
Paying your own way
Where you decide
No curfews

A job means
Defining yourself
Something you give in exchange
For something you need
Something you give
To fulfill your need to give
Something you do
That is worth your time
To make a difference
Somewhere in the world
Anywhere you can work

A job means
Taking on a new family
An extended network of colleagues
Future friends
Possible relatives
New faces and places
Minds waiting to dream
Empowering each other
With ourselves

A job means
Hope replacing hopelessness
Gearing up
Gathering momentum
Jumpin' on the train.

Dance with Me

by Sandra María Esteves

I need to spin
Like comet in air
Caught in atomic counterpoint
Of two becoming one
Held in the balance of delicate embrace
The way ocean caresses
Lays into sand
Where shorelines of naked melodies
Wait to invoke your sacred name

Play me into your arms
In sweet sambas and hot merengues
In the middle
Under stars
Where we become
The offering
The bamba
The prayer
The kata
The mandala
The mantra
El caracol
Brought to life

Spin me
Step to me
Into me
Around me
Like I'm there
In your arms
Thru your skin
Running in your blood

Hold me close
Tight and fearless
Moving
Like summer wind

In what love is
The music and dance
The bolero of being
Together

Sing me
Like spring flute
Over blue water
In conga cadence
Where feet levitate
Flying to sun

Fly me thru the air
Around and down
Born again
In the you and I
This now of us
Into each other
In salsa son
A song
In hip-hop cu-bop
A discovering
A finding
You radiate/I glow
In your light
Becoming

Dance me
Into your life
Into your many roomed house
Into mornings
Where you begin
Into the first page
In your new book of poems
Into your baños
Burning sage and prayer songs
Into San Lazaro rituals
Around your head
Healed again

142

Move me
By your open window
Of mountain and sky
Where the moon communicates
Her fullness

Hold me
As close as you can
So all I see is universe
Thru your eyes
And your breath becomes
My life-force
As I nest my wings
Onto your tree of life

Place me
Right there
At that point of focus
Where our souls rise
In perfect balance
Into brilliant colorful light

Dance with me
Again and again.

En Puerto Rico

by Sandra María Esteves

El mar te ama
The ocean loves you
Jumps up on you
Slaps your face
Kisses you all over the place
Welcomes you home
Doesn't matter who you are
Over and over
When you need this caring
You just come

As long as you
Watch out
Don't swim too far
Into unexpected undercurrents
Tangled into weeds

En Puerto Rico
The ocean truly loves you
Coqui symphonies in the dark
Curas de coco
Seashell parades
Wind in your hair
Sand all in your toes

Aye Papi, que bueno!
You fall in love again
Every time you return
Find yourself in the sun
Bless yourself in the rain
Heal yourself in the sea
Feeling into the you
Who you are meant to be.

Blues for Malcolm
by Sandra María Esteves

We are flower petal
Fragile to touch
Delicate to handle
Abuse from wind and rain
A destiny of inevitable tearing
Following thunderstorms

We are raindrops
Born of sky
Longing to come home
Return to ocean
Thru the river of life

We are moon
Appearing and dancing
Across heaven
In rumba to stars

We are wind that changes

When we wear our coat of dreams
We become tempered sword

We are gentle petal
Perfume in the rain
When wind lifts us
We become sword

We are silk
From cloth of light
To bless the earth
Like rose and lotus
A holy mix of coloring
Brilliant in the light

When we dare
To plant seeds

We become tempered sword

We mark a path
We are petal
Flower
Stylus and stamen
Leafy collar
Prickly stem
That roots to earth
Whenever our seeds
Are born from here
We are tempered sword

We are rainfall
Over open fields
Our father the mountain
Our mother the tree
Fruit of her branches
We bear witness
Celebrate life
We choose to be sword

In our cloth of light
We bless earth
Dance with moon
Sing into wind
We are petal
Flower
Rainfall and mountain

We Choose To Be Sword.

Untitled

by Sandra María Esteves

A poem is an incantation into the universe
That was born from the universe
Thru the voice of a poet

A poem is the universe singing
To itself

A poem is the breath of the universe
Inhaling into the poet
Like a gift

Even when it arrives angry
It is still a gift

A poem is the focus of things
A window just discovered
Where the sun always shines
And rain only falls when you need
To get wet

A poem says things you need to hear
Things you don't want to remember
But can't afford to forget

A poem does not lie, it is
A revelation

A poem is eternity
Expressing itself
In the music of this moment

A poem is like a member of your family
Who picks you up when you fall

When you are in need
The poem comes
It is there, awaiting you
Like a faithful lover
Whispering your name in the dark.

Howard Simon was born in the lake-front city of Cleveland, Ohio. He attended Morehouse College where he majored in Drama. Moving to New York City after college to pursue a theatre career, Howard appeared in several Off-Off Broadway productions, producing and directing two of his own plays. In fall 1995 he will attend the Dramatic Writing Program at New York University. For the WritersCorps, he worked at the Bronx Satellite Academy.

Photo by Wayne Providence

I wanted to work in the theater, to be an actor, so I came to New York, and I realized that what I really wanted was to be a "star." Of course, that never happened, and I had to regroup. I found what I enjoyed doing the most and was best at was writing, so I became a playwright. As a playwright, I get to create roles for friends, which is important to me. I admire someone like Spike Lee because he's always trying to bring new blood into the film business. I figured if I wrote plays and produced them myself, I could bring more work to people of color—in costume, lighting, set design, and acting.

My plays deal a lot with language. I like to play with words and the hidden meaning behind language. But I don't come up with words, I come up with characters. I really like my characters—what they say, and how they say it. Everybody I've written about has something to say—good, bad, indifferent—just like we all have something to say.

I'm not so sure if writing is all that important to the people who go to plays, as opposed to the action. The writing documents a time, but plays are written to be performed. You can read it, but once the director and actors put their mark on it, it can be a totally different thing from what you read—or what you wrote. I think that may be one of the problems with the genre: it leaves a lot of room for interpretation. Poems leave a lot of room also, but novels and stories are more concrete.

People need drama because it mirrors life, but more than that, it feeds the soul. When people see a play they get caught up in the moment, and begin to understand moments. It's like an out of body experience—you're experiencing the moment, at the same time you're looking at it, analyzing it, feeling it. I'm not sure that happens to us normally.

I'm a part of WritersCorps because, quite simply, this is what I should be doing at this point in my life. I'm in a transitional period, and WritersCorps fits right into that. When we started the program, I had produced two of my own plays, and was trying to decide where to go from there. Did I want to continue as a professional writer, or did I want to go to law school and make lots of money? WritersCorps came along and was one of the first organizations that solicited my material and offered me something because of my writing ability. That was a turning point, and so I decided I was going to stick with this.

I really had no expectations when I came to WritersCorps. All I knew was that it was a part-time job that had something to do with writing. Then when I got my first site—Schomberg Satellite Academy High School—I did have expectations, which was a problem, because my expectations did not fit their expectations. I had designed a project which involved the students writing a play, producing it, maybe even charging admission and making some money. My expectation was that they'd want to do something other than the regular old nothingness that they do. I don't mean "nothingness" in a negative way, because a lot of my students have complicated lives—so many things happening to them, both negative and positive. I wanted them to have a unique experience, but they weren't open to that, and that's sad. It's not only saddening, it's frightening.

I have no idea what the problem really is. I could say, "Oh, we have a school system that's failing us," or I can point a finger at other things, but there's still one important factor, and that is *self*. There is probably something within themselves that's limiting their possibilities. I sympathize with kids today, because I see myself in them. I see a lot of similarity in terms of economic and social status, and in terms of empowerment, but there was still something in me—maybe from my mom—that there is more to all this. I remember once reading in the newspaper about a woman at a local junior high school in Cleveland who took a group of children to Europe every year. All I knew about Europe was that it wasn't where I was and I wanted to go. Of course, we couldn't afford to go, but the drive was still there, the yearning for other places. This was important to me and was the factor that drove me to do more.

What I really want to say is, when are we going to stop saying "This is an issue, that is an issue?"—there are issues, of course, but we can achieve in spite of that, be the best we can be. It ain't a bed of roses for a whole lot of people in this country, but people still achieve.

I don't want people to say that the purpose of WritersCorps is literacy. We're not about literacy. We're here to foster writing, and an awareness of and appreciation for literature, but WritersCorps is primarily here—in a minute way, in the only way in which a democratic country feels it can—to support its artists, its writers. We don't get paid enough, but this is one way that this government can allocate funds for writers. Five thousand dollars isn't a lot, but it's a lot to a writer who has to do all kinds of things to make ends meet. Some may argue, "Then why be in this profession?" If we really put value to things, then the highest paid profession should be the educators, but it's exactly the opposite. So WritersCorps is a support for artists. In return, I provide a service—I give readings, run workshops—all of which fosters writing and literature. For that I get a measly check—birdseed. But then I need the birdseed.

from the Bronx Satellite Academy

Chain of Thoughts
by Joshua R.

Being a person of color means a lot to me. . .
I still have a lot to learn about my family. . .
and background to help me identify myself. . .
It's hard for my sisters and brothers to acheive certain. . .
goals,
getting an education,
taking care of a family,
or even playing a role in society. . .
people are feeling that they are oppressed
but not using their knoweldge to escape
from their enclosure.

Be strong to overcome this cruel but overzealous world.. . .
Only your choices and actions will determine your future.

Are Our Minds Enslaved?
An Essay by Dushaun T.

I think a lot of minds are enslaved. When I say enslaved I mean ignorant or blind to reality. The sad thing is, a lot of people don't realize they're enslaved.

For example, people are not taught their history in school. In school we learn the Whites invented most of America's inventions. Blacks are people of success and establishment. Therefore, in order to be successful you must camouflage with the White culture. But at the same time they're telling us we're not equal, and could never be White. This is the oppression to keep Blacks down.

Another example is the young Black youth is out killing each other everyday. If their minds weren't enslaved, they would know this is just what the White man wants. They set us up to kill each other. For example, it is scientifically proven, that when you put a large amount of animals together without the proper elements they need to survive, they go crazy. They commit suicide, acts of cannibalism, or murder. The same thing happens in the ghetto.

Materialism is another way to brainwash someone. Media makes it seem like you are nothing if you don't have money and clothes. If your brain was not enslaved, you would know clothes don't make you a better person. Your mind is enslaved if you kill someone for clothes. The White man put things into the market they wouldn't buy themselves. Then they watch us kill ourselves to get it.

In conclusion, I think Black people need to understand the strikes against them in society. Only then can we establish ourselves in society. I think Blacks have the ability to be strong and dominate in society. If we study our history and learn the system, we can break out of the boundaries they have us in.

Is TV Brainwashing Society?
An Essay by Joshua R.

Society is being brainwashed by TV. The government has found a way to get into the home viewers' minds without them knowing it. There are certain things that people don't think to ask, like is TV fiction or reality? Do the things on TV take part in your everyday life, or do certain things just stick out to you like a sore thumb? In this essay, you will hear my point of view on how TV influences people of every age group in our society.

TV shows society what the government and TV corporations want it to see. For example, TV and its cartoons influence kids for toys, cereals, clothing, leaving parents no choice but to purchase the item. Cartoons have other "side effects," meaning bad things for kids. Cartoons have a lot of violence, as well as unrealistic topics.

Another way that society gets intimidated is comedy shows, and their funny ways of experimenting with topics politically or governmentally. This especially affects teenagers. Comedy can make you feel cool about what the government is doing, but that is what the government wants, so that you/society, can find humor in the downfalls of today's nation.

The last example that I will use is the News. The News is used to blind adults to what's really going on around them. The News only shows information that the government approves of.

So with the government and TV corporations feeding you all this information, don't you think you are being led into feeling certain ways about social issues? These are things that have to be dealt with in the home. From Cartoons to Comedy to News, every stage of our life has been affected. Families should talk more to each other about the importance of reality. We must help each other recover from the blindness of TV.

Success: Becoming A Responsible Adult
An Essay by Steven G.

Becoming a responsible adult is not an easy task in life. You must work at becoming responsible each and every day. The road to becoming a responsible adult is a long and bumpy one.

There are many obstacles along the road to becoming a responsible adult that may sway a young and eager mind off their track. In most cases teenagers are required to take this journey alone. There are influences or obstacles which cause weak teenagers to disregard their responsibilities.

Influences such as illegal substances, the opposite sex, and peer pressure can be overwhelming. These things take time and effort away from the more important things in life.

154

I myself at one time chose to make independent irresponsible decisions which I paid the price for. In doing so, I have learned from many mistakes, and how to avoid making new ones. I realized that in life there are channels that you must go through in order to survive in today's world.

I now know that a responsible adult is one who sets his/her priorities. An example of this would be taking the steps to finish school in order to pursue a career. This is the start of becoming a responsible adult.

Setting your priorities and balancing our needs with our wants are keys to becoming a responsible person.

"The Choice"

An Essay by Jenine V.

What was done in the past to slaves (not just Black slaves) is a hard memory for certain races. Yet we choose not to forget, because even though we personally didn't go through it, it disturbs us and especially me. If the White people had so much authority, what makes us think they still don't? What if mentally we still are their slaves? It's a trick question but one we really have to think of.

A book named "The Miseducation of the Negro" describes a lot about what I am trying to explain. Except I feel as a Puerto Rican we all need to be recognized equally! A quote from the book has really made me realize more about our society. I would like to share it with you: "A minority's mind has been all but perfectly enslaved in that he has been trained to think what is desired of him." So as minorities we all struggle to accomplish and gain what the White man has earned. The majority of us tries to get ahead and get a good education. We are not offered the same education as upper class people. So right there we are being robbed. Another thing is in the business industry, this thing the government calls "minimum wage" is like another form of slavery. You work long hours and get little pay. Just because we are being paid doesn't make it okay! We should get paid good for the hard work we do.

To me it's like being held down; every little chance they get, they want to put us down. They don't want us to be successful, because then we will be equal. And this world we live in is run by mostly White people. When has there ever been a Puerto Rican or Black president? There hasn't because we haven't been given a chance. I feel they are afraid to give us a chance, because people who strived know how to stick it out and they might be good.

What needs to be done is live and let live. We need to recognize each other as people and not as color. Realize that we're really not that different. But in order to do that we have to speak, let our voices be heard and show that we're concerned. We will either make peace or destroy each other! Which one do you choose?

The Red House
on
The Red Clay Hill

An Excerpt from a play by Howard B. Simon

ACT I

> *It is late October of 1944. The place is Morehouse College in Atlanta, Georgia. The stage is divided into three playing areas. Stage right is the office of Dr. Mays, president of the college. Stage left is a dorm room. The elevated upper playing area is the chapel. There should only be a podium in the upper playing area. As the house lights are lowered the quartet lines a hymn. "A charge to keep I have. A God to glorify."*

> *(Lights rise on chapel. Day. Mays is finishing his weekly morning address to the men of Morehouse in the chapel.)*

MAYS. And so I tell you young men my life was in danger on that train as I tried to defy segregated laws that are unjust and immoral. I don't quite know what I'm going to do about it right now. Some say that I should bring charges against the Southern Railway, and others say I should do nothing that might cause difficulties here at this fine Negro College. But I do know that you as young men must grow and become good citizens. Never believe an unjust law that tries to make you believe that you are less than a man who deserves respect. Never let anyone define who you are. You are God's children. Let us bow our heads in prayer. Let us pray for all the brave soldiers who at this time are engaged in serious battle across the sea. May God bring a speedy and just end to this war. For God is the only one who can put an end to all wars.

(The Morehouse Quartet sings "Ride On King Jesus." The lights fade on the chapel and come up on the dorm room. Four young men enter. They are members of the Quartet.)

SKINNY. Hey, Pop, did you finish your chemistry assignment?

ODELL. I hope all of you gentlemen have finished your assignments. They are due in about fifteen minutes.

BUD. Look, we don't want to hear you and your self righteous preaching this morning. Can you help me with a few of the answers, Pop?

POP. I've finished all of them except the last one. You can see them while I work on the last one.

ODELL. All three of you can forget it.

POP. Why do you say that?

ODELL. Because that problem will take at least thirty minutes to finish and as of now we have twelve minutes to class.

SKINNY. Pop can do this problem in no time with no trouble.

ODELL. You may not believe this, but even I had trouble with this problem, and I went to professor yesterday. He told me that the problem should take at least thirty minutes to solve.

BUD. Just because you're always up in professor's backside and always get the highest grade in the class doesn't make you the smartest one in the class. I have faith in Pop, and I bet that he finishes the problem before class with the right answer.

ODELL. I bet one dollar that he doesn't.

BUD. You're on. Skinny, are you finished with numbers one through six?

ODELL. One through six, there were only seven problems on the assignment. You mean to tell me that you didn't do any of the problems?

BUD. Yes, I didn't do any of the problems.

SKINNY. None?

BUD. Look, don't you start either. You're copying too.

SKINNY. Yes but I only want answers to two of the problems. You want *all* the answers.

BUD. Copying is copying whether it's two or all the problems.

ODELL. He's right for once. I can't believe you are copying.

BUD. You can't? Watch.

ODELL. I'm surprised that you would copy, Skinny. That is no way to prepare for medical school.

BUD. *(Mimicking)* "I'm surprised, I'm surprised." You talk too much.

ODELL. I can expect you to cheat because you have to, but I'm disappointed when Skinny or Pop cheats.

BUD. What does that mean?

ODELL. It just means that we received good basic training at the Palmer Normal School. I expect more from them. I do realize that you received what type of education you could get. How you were accepted into this college I don't know, but I guess even this college is entitled to one good deed.

BUD. *(He jumps up ready to fight.)* Listen, I've had about enough of you. . .

POP. Finished.

SKINNY. Yes. Give me my dollar.

ODELL. Wait, let me see the answer. *(POP shows him the answer.)* I can't believe it. How did you do it?

BUD. He's smarter than you, that's all.

158

ODELL. What would you know about smart, Mr. can't read? *(BUD grabs ODELL and SKINNY pulls BUD away. POP is trying to calm ODELL down.)*

POP. Odell, just calm down, and stop provoking Bud.

ODELL. Provoking? He was the one who didn't know the word "expeditious" in class yesterday.

BUD. Oh yeah? Watch me expeditiously whoop your behind.

SKINNY. Listen, we've got five minutes to get to class, and we all know how professor feels about tardiness.

POP. Yeah, we better get to class. Odell, how did you feel about Dr. Mays' talk this morning?

BUD. I think he oughta press charges against the railroad.

ODELL. He asked me, and no, I think he should just forget about the whole incident.

SKINNY. Forget about it?

POP. What about the shameful way they treated Dr. Mays?

BUD. You should be ashamed for thinking like that.

ODELL. Mr. Southerland, who is on the Board of Trustees, is advising Dr. Mays to restrain his comments for the good of the college.

SKINNY. For the good of the college? To say or do nothing says that the college believes it's OK to walk all over the Negro.

POP. And if I know Dr. Mays as we all know him, that is not going to happen.

ODELL. You fail to realize one important factor, and that is

Morehouse College is in desperate need of money.

BUD. You don't know what you're talking about and neither does Mr. Southerland. What does he know?

ODELL. He knows enough. That's why he's on the Board of Trustees, and you're a cotton picking farm boy who can't half read.

(BUD goes after ODELL. SKINNY and POP are barely holding him back.)

SKINNY. Odell, shut the hell up.

POP. Yeah, go on to class.

ODELL. Why? I didn't do anything.

BUD. That's right you ain't done nothin. Yaw can stop holding me. I ain't gonna hurt the damn fool.

ODELL. I think you're the fool.

BUD. Put it this way. I come from a farm. We don't pick cotton as you believe, but it's a farm. Only difference between you and me is that I know what the White man is about. Me and my family we know how the White man mistreats the Negro, but we don't let it into our minds and souls. But you, on the other hand, you kiss all up behind the White man and he still mistreats you. You grin and shuffle in the White man's face, and you're still a Nigger in his eyes. Now who's the fool?

ODELL. You can say what you want, but. . .

POP. But we need to get to class.

(Lights fade on dorm room, and rise on Dr. Mays' office.)

SADIE. Ben, you didn't eat breakfast this morning. So I've come to walk you home for lunch.

160

BEN. What did you cook for lunch?

SADIE. Well, I fried some corn and I baked some cornbread. And I can warm the fried chicken that was left from dinner last night.

BEN. You got a deal. Let me sign a couple of documents, and I'll be right with you, Mrs. Mays. (*He goes to his desk and begins to sign documents.*)

SADIE. Ben, what is this name that the boys are now calling you?

BEN. Buck Benny.

SADIE. Buck Benny?

BEN. Yes, the boys got it from the Jack Benny Show. Buck is a hero character that saves the day.

SADIE. I like it. It fits you.

Jesús Papoleto Meléndez is a performance poet and recipient of a COMBO(Combined Arts of San Diego)-NEA Fellowship in literature. He is creator of the jazz/poetry quartet *Exiled Genius,* and has performed in festivals nation-wide. A native of New York City, his published works include 4 books of poetry, most recently *"Concertos on Market Street,"* (Kemetic Images Press, 1993), and appear in 15 literary journals and anthologies, including *"Paper Dance"* and *"Unsettling America."* As a WritersCorps member he conducted poetry workshops at Community Elementary School 235, Rafael Hernandez.

Photo by Wayne Providnece

I am a writer because when I was very young, I discovered that there were all sorts of ideas and story lines running through my mind that needed to be expressed. What fascinated me most was the fact that I could close my eyes and see a movie—a movie I'd never seen. I didn't know the people in it, but I knew what they were going to say, what they were feeling, and what was going to happen.

People always ask me, "Who was your literary influence?" I say, Mickey Mouse. When I was a kid in the fifties, TV was a new adventure. I watched a lot of TV, and my favorite show was Mickey Mouse—the cartoon. Sometimes I would watch the screen, and instead of images, I'd see the words that described those images, and began to write them down. I noticed that if I sat still, the words would come.

When I teach, I always begin with that same idea of stream of consciousness, because, for me, that's where writing comes from. If you read any writer's body of work, you'll find a thread—something they're always writing about—and as they evolve, so does that thread. George Orwell, for instance, is known for his comments on society, because that's what he cared about. We write from that place which embodies our vision, our beliefs, our upbringing, and from memories we've distorted.

Certain segments of society know they need writers, others don't, and others need to control that freedom of expression. Writers throughout history have been murdered, have had their tongues cut out—starting with Socrates, because his government didn't like what he had to say. Repressive governments, this one included, put writers away. In this country, writers and artists get busted for drugs, which makes them criminals instead of political prisoners. That's one way of shutting people down.

When we go into the schools as writers, the kids don't know that they need us. Once we begin to reveal ourselves to them, and make them aware of how we function—they realize that there's something they can connect with—they tune in. Sometimes when I walk into a classroom and the students are told they're having a poet today, they say "Ugh!" But once I get into my routine and they see that this is different from school, their attitudes change.

Unless we have a balance between art and sciences in the schools, we're going have a lopsided society, one that's culturally crippled. For instance, it took a long time for people to realize that Africans and the history of Africa was that of emperors and empresses, dynasties and empires—for people to stop thinking of Cleopatra as Elizabeth Taylor. She wasn't—she was someone else, like Oprah. The school system keeps complaining that the kids have no role models, but won't allow role models to come into the classroom: there are no programs in the public schools that allow artists to go in and work.

There are lots of things wrong with WritersCorps. I don't like the salary: stipend or not, it isn't volunteer work if they take taxes out of it. What I do like is that WritersCorps is a program that gives us an opportunity to go into the schools to impart something that has been dormant. Poetry rises, because poetry has existed before the pencil, because life is in fact poetic and artistic. If you go back to the caveman, when somebody saw something they couldn't explain, they drew it so other people could grasp it. In order to explain the world around them, they had to communicate with one another. In a way, WritersCorps promotes that same thing.

With my students, I wanted to provide a holistic sense of what writing was about. We go into the schools to teach kids how to write—so what? They write a poem. How many of them show it to their mothers, their fathers, their brothers, the guy on the block? Most people, as I did, write poetry and keep it to themselves. It wasn't until I decided to become a public poet, that I discovered people were interested in what I had to say. That's what I'm trying to get across, to say—"Look, if you write a poem about committing suicide, you'll demystify that to the person sitting next to you, who is the same age as you." They'll each begin to understand that they're not alone in those feelings—that these are common feelings—and that empowers them to not jump out of the window.

The biggest problem these kids have is that their vantage point is limited. Their world is limited to the streets they cross, so how can they know where they're going? These kids have a great need.

I wanted to use computers with my kids, because their facility to understand technology is there, and they're fascinated by computers, but they never get to play with them. I wanted to teach them, not just how to write, but what to do with their work after they write: how to make a book that they could give to their friends and family, who will read it and get enlightened. I wanted to show them the entire process, but because I didn't have these tools in my school, I had to bring the poems home, and do the work on my own computer.

I knew if I taught them about computers in addition to writing,

165

they'd start writing on their own, just to use the computer. If they each had their own computer, they could go into their files and see their poems; they could do the anthology themselves. We're not trying to manufacture writers—we're here to help young people find out who they are, what their possibilities are, their potential.

There It Is Always a Morning
by Rosalina R.

A morning for me is always a special Morning Day.
Because it is a day that has love, fun, and happiness.
However, when there is a morning there is love,
    when there is a morning there is happiness.
So we always need to have a Morning Day.
            EVERY DAY AND TIME!!!!!!!!

You're Always in My Heart
by Rosalina R.

Every time I remember you,
You are in my heart,
You and only you always will be in my heart.
Because I am going to remember you always
    DAY AND NIGHT AND EVERY TIME!!!!

ME
by Rosalina R.

Me is me,
I wish I could be a model,
Me is me because God made me like that.
Me is me,
And always will be me.

The Book
by Amanda R.

The book is me
the book has
a volume
The book travels
from here to there
fast and slow
The book that
I like is the
best. The book.

167

My Mother

by Amanda R.

My mother is
the person
who brought me
into
this world
she could
also
take me
out
I get
upset
when she
gets me
mad
but
I still
love her
and that
makes me
glad.

That Sky

by Amanda R.

That sky
that looks white
that sky that blows
my mind. That sky
ain't it so big
Next comes the
 Angels
The Angels in
Heaven in
that sky.

Within My Hands

by Stacy Leigh P.

The thing that I see in my hand
is the letter X, M and a N.
I see, like a dark red and a white.
I know that the dark red means
probably the hard times in
school, and probably the
white means the good times
that I had in school.
I also could do a lot with my hands
like hold, touch, pull and
tug. That's all I see.

Gangs

by Stacy Leigh P.

Gangs, Fighting,
and shooting.
Why is this in our world?
Gangs, Fighting and shooting.
Tell me why this is in our world?
People getting their props.
Why?
I don't know.

My Life

by Pedro R.

I do not
Like my life because
You know I go to
A lot of places
At one
Time that is
Number 1
But it
Is getting pretty good so far
I met some kids
I have some girls that
Like to talk to me.

Soul

by Rafael C.

My soul.
    The gift of life
          is

precious.
    It is the second
          life

I have
    when I die.
        My soul

is so precious.
      The gift
        of

life.
    So do not fear
        for
          your

first life,
      for
        you have a second.

Human Wisdom

It is important
              to keep
                        culture,
         Culture is The Essence
                        of Life,
         It's life itself....

The Story of Peoples'
              ways —
How they made
    their way
              in Life,
to deal with life,
    to understand it,
         their understanding
              cultivated
                   in
         this wisdom,
passed on,
         through
              children
                   for Ever....

    Their ancient cries,
                   the moans
              of Living
                        Souls,
              reLiving
         a past,
    a part
    a being of
         themselves,

    removed

         & yet contained
                   within

                itself....

Some People lay
            eXtinct,
         their way
            unknown,
   the Sum
         of their
            eXistence
      as erased
         as footsteps
            in the sand;
Some People are
            as dead
         as dead
         can be
            dead,

Their memory
      (the memory
            of them)

                  disappeared
         from memory
               itself —

      No one left of it
               to speak for it —
   Not a soul
            alive
               to weep for its dead,
                           Its Sacrifice.

This,
      That is in the breasts
                  of Women,
            in the Womb
               itself,
                     in the water
                        where sperm

swims

innate,
this wisdom

Like the cool
and demure flower,
forcing its way
through earth
to the light of
day,
to see the Sun;
to place its blooming face
before it (

beyond the Eons
of Time &
Space)

, rooted in
this unknown
place
to which
we give a foreign name
as meaning just the same
Wherever we
are standing
there,
Celebrating
the distinctive
cultures
of a man
which
make us
common men.

Closing the 20th Century

We no longer need a Sanitation Dept
                              :the homeless
                                    are out
        in the God-forsaken
                    dead hours
                          of the night,
                                  looking thru
                          garbage cans,
                                    rearranging
        the discarded belongings
                        of a society....

In New York City
            they lay
                  all the garbage out
                        along the sidewalks
                              & sell us
                  whatever we want to buy back;
                                  used Gillette Razor Blades,
                        an old toothbrush with stains,
                        assorted screws,
                                old magazines,
                        last week's t.v. guide,
                                    & the news;
          a once button-down sweater
            with a hole
                  in its sleeve
                        lays languidly,
          its intricately
            crocheted
              embroidery
                        goes
            largely ignored;
                        wrinkled up
                        subway maps,
                              — AnyThing

174

they find
  in the street, back
      to the street
         they return it,
           like meticulous
             ants
               of too-human
                 dreams & desires;

They crush soda cans,
        collect bottles & glass,
  boxes & newspapers,
          rags, mopsticks, &
             brooms
       all through
        with
          the work
       of their lives;
Old,
 beatup men and women
   are beating the children
      at the mischief
       of scavenger hunts —
            No Truth is left
              for the youth
           to uncover;

The trash cans are empty
  when the sanitation workers
      arrive,
        they are light,
      so their
         load
      for
      this night,
 as their contents, as conscience
     litter the streets
      like lost children
        LooKing
         for cigarettes

& sleep;

In dank and dreary rainy April afternoons,
              when *Spring*
                    is about
              to open its mouth,
                          & the Earth
                    is Fecund
              with the flowers of Life,
                    the garbage
                                            sails
    along the gutters,
              around the corners
                    of every neighborhood,
                          aCross, The American Way
    &
    sinks
          into democratic sewers
              where its influence flows
                    throughout
                          the rest
                                of the world....

Tourism Up/Dow Jones, 6pts.

Welcome to San Diego!
(Now Go Home!!!) Say
    theBumperstickers ,Last Stop
             in the u.s.
               of.a.

Where
  the driving civilian population
               has the freeway
        To run over Mexican
            Illegal
            Aliens
               on the HighWay,   All
               on the Run
                  trying to escape
                     their native tongue

      To find a decent job
       in a land
         where they
           can't speak
             a Word
         of the
           language
             The People
               use there
          to abuse Them;
                 I've seen Them:
Lying dead
 On the sides of the road;
            The road to Mexico,
            The road to San Diego
   wrapped in blankets
   of finer cloths
     than the rags of their own clothes;
                It is this way,
                It is this way....

These UnNumBereD
   OutNumBereD
   OutLaWeD
        Hard Workers
   Become DoCuMenTeD
        Dead People
            in the morgue
            of a strange world,
                    truly forgotten.

Juan Gómez Quiróz was born in Chile. A US citizen, he was awarded a Fulbright fellowship for Painting at Yale University, an NEA, and a Guggenheim Fellowship. His paintings are held in the permanent collections of the Museum of Modern Art, the Guggenheim, and Metropolitan Museum of Art in New York. He is currently working on two novels *"The Desolation Files"* and *"Three Chronicles of Spoken Literture."* For the WritersCorps he conducted a workshop for Spanish writers at the Longwood Arts Center in the South Bronx, and published the workshop anthology, *"Espacio de Escritores."*

Photo by Raoul Sentenat

My story is the story of being an artist. It's the most difficult path a human being can take. To be a part of any movement and add to culture is a very difficult task. I was a painter before I was a writer, and to create an image for me was to paint the world around me. Then it was not enough—I wanted to tell people a story, and writing was the only way I could get to them. What amazes me about writing is being able to tell something that you really feel, and to entertain.

When I was young, I wanted to be a pilot, but I couldn't because of my eyesight. I decided to be an artist, because my father had a bar and I saw that being an artist was easier than being a merchant. It took me years to learn how to express myself as a painter, to come up with my own style, and to be recognized.

I was very lucky to come from Chile, and I grew up among writers. I met Neruda, and was part of the School of Fine Arts where there were always writers who made me think of a poem as a very abstract way to convey an idea, that in few words you have to say something—just as with color.

Artists talk a lot—and that's also what brought me to writing, because everybody told me stories and I liked to listen. Living in New York, in Soho, I began writing short stories. Then I put them all together into a novel. This is the novel I'm working on now—about a conversation between a poet and a painter. They are always asking each other, "What's more abstract—color or words? Is language—the sound of the language—as abstract as color? What is more difficult—to paint a tree or to describe it in a poem?"

The good thing about WritersCorps was that I was able to read aloud. Reading my work aloud transformed me. When you're painting, there's no one there to tell you if it's finished or not, or if they like it. After I read for the first time in public, people applauded! Painters don't have this satisfaction.

WritersCorps was also a challenge for me because I had never met other Spanish language writers in the US. There were very few people here I could relate to as a writer in my own language, because people didn't give me credibility as a writer—they gave me credibility as a painter. There were no workshops in Spanish at a certain level. WritersCorps gave me the opportunity to have my own workshop, and it's amazing that I'm able to work with twelve very devoted Spanish writers.

I put the group together through a Spanish newspaper ad! These are poets and people who have come from very oppressive situations. Their way of seeing things and expressing themselves is very new to me. Every Saturday we read and have a great time; we listen to each other, and we are learning from each other.

WritersCorps has provided these people with something that they didn't have before—a place to read their work, and respect for each other. I'm talking about people who were walking in the street, who found the newspaper in the rain—people who wanted to write something. I have a Mexican writer who comes all the way from New Jersey for our workshop. We have writers from prison who also read about us in the newspaper, who contacted me, and now we have a workshop with them by mail. So we are also providing a service for people unfortunate enough to be in prison.

The discipline and the respect you get from other writers—that has been very good for me. I am also able to offer them my knowledge of computers, which they don't have. It's going very well. I really like what I do. We are also preparing a workshop anthology, and we will be participating in the Hostos College Fair. So the group is really getting together to provide a service. They each have the pleasure of working in their native language. That's what we are providing, and it has been very fulfilling for all of us.

Untitled
by Hector Ruizdiaz

a bonfire is blazing

it is the bonfire of recent loves

it discharges a load of the forgotten,

all love is in the beginning dry fire

abstruse games

a sword that opens a wound in the stone.

A Poem
by Lydia Walteros

I am part of what I was
of the past made present
bee, flower, child
a little of all

I adorned my hair
with wild flowers
closed my eyes
with the free melody of the birds

I let the wind caress me
the sun love me
accompanied or alone
my feeling was the same. . .

searching for truths
I obtained fantasies
I became a woman.

A Poem
by Christine Perez

I know of an endless tunnel of hazy grey walls,
with mazes of lugubrious rooms,
with an asphyxiating putrid atmosphere.
I know of a funereal tunnel buried within my soul.

182

A Picture San Francisco
by Jorge A. Valdes

a man in a barbershop in
San Francisco.
W. Saroyan

a solitary man
San Francisco

accidentally I arrived to The Earth

We were three little brothers   surprised
of every little detail of this century
time of duration of the Summers
distance between my feet and the airplanes

in the afternoon We used to drink coffee
and eat bread among people dead by now

that way my life passed and today I remember
grandmother scattering bread in the barns
my brother among The Beatles
the years sixties

sometimes I confuse The Summers

a solitary man anywhere
has much to do with what I think
it is just a certain picture where I am
and one of these Summers I won't be

then   who is going to tell my parallel
when I won't be here and I too
will be a spot staring at the new century

they will say that for being absent I forgot
the specifications   they will never know
that it was all a lie   nothing existed
except this emptiness in which We believed
but which sometimes was also truth
and the world was certainly our world
with its umbrellas and with its railroads

replica of a gigantic picture
whose main advantage is the reasoning
and this desire that God exists

close to the point of disappearing
I began to dream everything again
the whole world seemed to fit into a picture
and I started to measure from my feet.

Live

by Dixon Abreu

seer among virginal mysteries of the clock
lighting with his hands the moon
she lives dead before the loud darkness of her gaze
witness to the miserable worth
she avoids for the first time the beginning of her night

Three Chronicles of Spoken Literature

A Novel by Juan Gómez Quiróz
This is a Fragment

My name is Braulio Vivanco, a writer by vocation, a newspaperman by necessity. I have been working with the United Press International out of New York City for sometime now. I met Rodrigo Quiroga on a trip to Santiago, Chile, a few years ago while attending a show of his painting. They were clear abstracts with a fearful, yet strong statement about light and color. I had not seen such good painting in a long time, even in New York or Paris, and told him as much.

He invited me to his studio, where we talked for hours. I found Rodrigo to be as good a listener as a story teller; he is well-read in fiction and sciences, especially the new physics, dealing in his favorite subjects, Time and Space. These scientific texts provide a means for him to relate the natural beauty of his native Chile to his artistic work: the Andes mountains, volcanoes, earthquakes, lakes, jungles, the Pacific Ocean, and Antarctica. His paintings were abstract, and so was his language. When he expressed himself, using dense images as painters often do, I felt the verse and lyricism of poetry.

I am a novelist, and prose is a different way altogether to express Time and Space and abstract emotions, as to the technique needed, and the difference between a short story and a novel, beginning with the amount of pages necessary to tell the story. We have been arguing about the difference and quality of expression between writers and painters, and the artist's craft in general, ever since.

Rodrigo arrived in New York with a Guggenheim fellowship in painting. He looked at me and said, "I wish to stay here and paint in this city where the best school of painting is happening." He added that he discovered early on, that great painting and important art movements always happened far away: in another language and in developed countries. I said to myself, "He is young and inexperienced, yet he has the balls and determination of his artistic opinions, which he ferociously defended—the essential ingredient to make it in this country of cowboys."

My prediction for Rodrigo Quiroga was right. He became an important international artist of the sixties, and an important member of the New York School of Painting. His shows sold out in the galleries, and he won prizes in the Biennials.

185

Today we both live in Soho, and often meet at Puffy's, a tavern in Tribeca and the local artist's watering hole. I don't know why I started taping our conversations. Maybe it was because I carry a tape recorder, just like he carries his sketch pad. During one of those afternoons at Puffy's, we decided to make a book of natural transcriptions, improvising freely. The spoken word is an experimental form, using only the sound of language. There was no paper, no ink, no written symbol. The narrator told the story, just as Scherazade in "One Thousand and One Nights." In this case, Rodrigo told the story, his voice with its sound and modulation, in conjunction with the meaning of the words, were all part of the story. He was an actor, transforming the reader into a participant, or at least, a listener.

Now I've given you, reader, this explanation because the craft of being an artist is very interesting to Rodrigo and me. Please understand, that it is not a very commercial idea, and that few readers are going to be crazy about it, except for a couple of hard core gallery owners, and a few editors. But I do believe that the public has a genuine interest in finding out what an artist thinks, how he becomes one, and what makes an artist, whether it be a painter, writer or composer. So I continue with a sample of our conversation.

RODRIGO. What material is more difficult for expressing oneself? In mastering the language to find the Power of the Word to write a story in a book, or manipulating the images in the head and translating them into color, with materials like oil, to paint a picture, or mastering sounds and instruments for a Symphony to a tree? Which of these is more abstract and harder to master? Color, or sound or words, and which is more universal?

BRAULIO. I think I understand what you mean. Writing uses the symbols and sounds of a particular language, and that limits the understanding because the culture that goes with it can be Spanish or English. Yes, Color and Sound are used by the painter and the musician, and in that sense they are more abstract, and the understanding of sound is more universal—music reaches the audience's sensibility. So it's Color . . . in that case, I agree.

Another time we were at Puffy's sipping some beer, and I observed that after a few drinks, Rodrigo liked to compare people's behavior to situations. Today was no exception.

186

RODRIGO. Why is it that in Paris, the Arts are so clean and organized and without energy, unlike New York? In Chile you drink for a few cents and eat fruit that has taste. Here they have no taste. In New York, like in Santiago, the poets are a bunch of lazy people, compared to painters and sculptors.

BRAULIO. Yes, and why is that?

RODRIGO. Look—they don't need a large space to paint and keep their work, or pay a lot of rent. They write in the cafe and don't need to carry heavy materials, like canvas, or build stretcher bars and frames to carry paintings around—just a notebook, and now you see them with those little powerful computers—that's all they need.

BRAULIO. Don't be so critical of cerebral things. Any artist has to know when his shoes are too tight or comfortable on his feet—in other words, what kind of materials are best to work with. It's not a matter of ego or effort. It's a matter of aesthetic and taste, my dear Goya.

The conversation ended there, but on another occasion, when I had been waiting for him for hours in Puffy's, using the time for reading and proofing my new novel, Rodrigo arrived in bad humor. Sitting down, he started to draw on the tablecloth with his black wax crayon.

RODRIGO. My dear writer friend, I just saw a show that convinces me once more that painters are better writers, than writers are painters.

BRAULIO. No way. You just want to cover being late with that lousy statement. *(Laughing)*

RODRIGO. No, no. This has been bothering me for a long time. I'm saying this because I just saw a show of paintings by D.H. Lawrence and Henry Miller, and they are "stinkos." If you compare their work with the <u>*Noa Noa*</u> of Gauguin, and the theatre of Picasso, and the letters of Van Gogh, and Delacroix's Journal...yes painters can write. . .

187

BRAULIO. Excuse the interruption but, look here, dear maestro, survival as a writer is more difficult than that of the painter. It's far more difficult to have a novel published, than to sell a painting in the hundreds of galleries in New York. Now, if you think it's so easy, why don't you write a short story? The only thing I demand from you is that it's amusing, entertaining, and nothing I've heard before.

RODRIGO. I can, but I don't like to sit and write. I don't have the time. Painting is more direct for what I have to say.

BRAULIO. *(Laughing)* You are just lazy, and you are the one calling the poets lazy.

Rodrigo laughed with me then said seriously:
I'm a professional worrier, as you know, and I'm alarmed by the pollsters saying that young people don't read. They prefer to watch television. And in undeveloped countries, people get their informa-tion from TV. Not only dictators exploit the media, but here in America, the news is manipulated by right-wing interest groups. It's appalling to me. Newspapers are being replaced by the Ten O'clock News, and videos do the rest. Remember Nero said, while Rome was burning: "To the people. . .Bread and Circus. Nowadays it seems to me it's "To the people, Drugs and MTV."

Then and there we decided to create this book to alarm the public of the danger of losing the power of freedom that the written word carries, as people and culture are being replaced by porno magazines and TV violence as the entertainment for the masses— produced by the CD ROM crowd—glorifying crime and self-destruc-tive behavior. And so I transcribed these conversations little by little, to make these pages, creating dialog, and sometimes inventing text. So, my dear reader, come and join us on this literary trip. Here we go.
(Pause followed by the sound of muted voices at the bar. Jazz plays in the background: John Coltrane or Thelonious Monk Quartet.)

BRAULIO. Tape one. . . Rodrigo. . . Action.

RODRIGO. *(Nervous voice, firm and clear after a few lines)* I have thought a lot about these three stories. The first one is about the revelation to me of artistic talent. The second one is about the political and social commentary that goes on around you when you are deciding what you want to be, and the third one is about a collector and the power of his possessions which led him to Evil.

The first one I call, "The Penknife." As a prologue, I have to say that I originally divided this story into six sequences like chapters. Now, however, they come together, because with the years, I realized that each sequence was a buoy en route to the salvation and security of a lost sailor, shipwrecked on a troubled and stormy sea.

(He Pauses)

Now you see I am fat and balding. But when I was fifteen, I had long blonde hair, and was muscular and handsome—the star of the soccer team in high school. All these attributes I owe to my Spanish grandparents. They came from Burgos in Castilla, the land of El Cid. Mr. Rodrigo Quiroga and Mrs. Teresa Bravo were wine makers. They came to the New World to plant a new vineyard and raise children. They had eleven, and settled in Talagante, not far from Santiago. On my mother's side, I have Mr. Luis Tapia and Mercedes Maulén, typical Chileans from Los Andes, a town that looks like it is hanging from the high mountain peaks, always covered with eternal snow.

(He Pauses.)

Cut. Time out. I need a drink.

(Short Pause. Braulio's voice in the firm tone of a director)

BRAULIO. Tape two. Start any time you want.

Ana Ramos is pursuing her BA in Psychology at CUNY, Hunter College, has studied classical ballet and has worked as an actress. In the 1970s, she was a founding member of the Puerto Rican artists' collective, New Rican Village. She has been Artist-in-Residence in the San Diego City Schools, and has worked in live television production throughout New York City. For WritersCorps, she conducted workshops at junior high and middle schools in the South Bronx.

Photo by Wayne Providnece

191

I write to communicate. Having lived on this planet for a while, what I've learned as a human being is that life is a contradiction, that there are going to be challenges and obstacles. So I write to confront life, to keep myself from going crazy. I don't necessarily write to be read. I've been a dancer, an actress, a television producer, and they're all ways for me to deal with life artistically.

Society doesn't think that it needs writers—doesn't realize that everything begins as a thought, which in turn becomes a physical manifestation. The next step is taking that pen and paper and working out that thought process—the creative act. We write to make a shopping list, directions, a math problem. We write to maintain, preserve, document, and finally, communicate.

We have begun to disregard our imagination because the modes of communication are making the written word obsolete. Working in television, I know that a story must be a three-minute or two-and-a-half-minute piece, and that the sidebars are supposed to augment that story. Everything has to be done fast, which is both good and bad. Writing as a creative act brings so many personal issues into play you become committed to it. Then it's read and someone else gets fired up, and your feelings are reborn again.

WritersCorps keeps me from being unemployed, for one thing. Then going into these schools I found that it was a way for me to reclaim some lost ground. I graduated high school in 1969 and several of my friends from that time have died of a drug overdose— and that was out of Catholic school. In those days, dark skinned people were looked upon as savages. So I knew the odds were stacked against these kids. Then coming into the school I saw a hundred of me!

I don't know if my project was successful, because I don't know if I've had a lasting effect. Some kids came through with work for the anthology, with me badgering them. Then some were writing on their own who didn't need badgering. I would hope that these kids have learned how to listen to what's inside them, and to what's going on around them, and not take things for granted.

WritersCorps is an opportunity for people who have been out in the world to offer kids a break, a different slant on things, to let them know that they have to find out who they are, to carve out their own place in the world. The mission of WritersCorps should be to nurture and instill respect in others for their own minds. When you respect your mind it's a step toward independence, and independence is a step toward true freedom, and freedom allows you to choose things in life. You can be revolutionary using federal funds.

Ana Ramos

from JHS 149, Elijah D. Clark and
I.S. 183, Paul Robeson Magnet School

The Talking Coconut is Talking to Me
for Jorge Brandon

by Ladia L.

The talking coconut is talking to me,

You were more than a shadow
walking in the street,
You were alive, with a heartbeat,
you breathe the same breath
as all, with your strife, through everything
you breathed the breath of life,

You were something not easy to be
seen,
You were a body with a heart
so clean,
You were someone with something
to share
You were the breath of life
the breath of love and care,

Under the stars is where you slept
but yet your heart never wept
is there a Trouble?
What can it be?

El coco que habla;
Please speak to me.

Everlasting Light

by Glorimar G.

In the presence of this candle
I see Everlasting life and birth
Looking into it
I see evil
But it expresses to me
that there is hope in my life
I see laughter of birth
and
sadness in death
Just to think
that there is a beginning and an end to life

194

and I'm just beginning
My heart is still beating
I am young
and I have strength
and I know
that in my imagination I see
that my life does not end
until my life candle
stops burning.

Moonlight Stalker
by Anthony P.

The moon tumbles down the Horizon
Death comes instantly
Do we remember the pain
No
only the sun matters now
Its light hits us mesmerizing us
making us forget the pain
that was once here
In an instant we forget
or maybe it's down there
waiting
waiting for the next night
and then we will forget the pleasure
of the sun and go back to the pain
that always comes back no matter
how hard we try to hide it
it will always come Back!

If the World Would Only Be Quiet
by Dennis B.

When I lay down
I always duck
Because in front of my building
they go
buck
buck
buck
I dropped a piece of bun
My mother said run
because a boy got a gun
I thought it was my gut BUT
it was only a cut on my butt
He don't want no riot
all me and Rodney want is the
World to be Quiet

The Way A Candle Light Burns
by Pedro C.

The way the wick of a candle
burns
is the way the
inside of my heart burns
As I see the way the death of a loving mother can go out
so quick
just like the way the candle flame
goes out so quick

The pain is burning inside me
seeing a loved one
die is like seeing a candle
burn out

It is hopeless and empty
I wish my mother could live forever
just like I wish a candle
would never burn out

Deep In The Mirror
by Divine G.

When I look at my eyes
I see no truth,
just horrible lies
on the outside I look brave
and strong but,
on the inside I cry,
all day long
I'm just a coward
hiding my feelings
from the world
All my friends are dying,
I'm afraid that I might be next.

Wildlife

by Ana Ramos

I saw a bunny in the Bronx, a white
little bunny rabbit, eating the dried
weeds no other animal could eat on
White Plains Road

The tough dirty little bunny didn't
pay any attention to me even when I
crouched down, watching it munch
away, eye to eye

A tough little bunny white, grayed
hanging in there, a survivor, sticking
out the winter in a lot with rundown
vehicles I look at and think junk
abandoned

So beautiful, what a shock, this tiny
furry, out of place, perhaps escapee
from a pet shop, perhaps an Easter
gift too wild even for the projects to
deal with, this crazy rabbit, so cute so
cuddly, quietly grazed with serious
appetite

Yeah, so I saw this bunny on the
street all by itself, small like a baby
little smudges on its body and little
face, biting and chomping at yellow
little sticks, no carrots

Big black eyes perfectly round
focused away far ahead of itself
looked like it was doing one thing -
eating - but seeing something else
altogether unrelated to the grass

I expect to see a rabbit in the country
miles away from this city sidewalk
but it is here, stops me in my tracks
thinking that any loud noise
and it would run off, but no

So I continue to walk but slowly
toward it, crouch down to watch it
close up, straight in the face
The bunny doesn't budge, it's not
paying attention to me at all
My presence doesn't deter the bunny
from what it is doing: Eating
And it continues to keep doing what it
is doing: Eating
My being there doesn't matter, at all
And then I get up, keep walking on
I turn to look back to see if it is still
there and
the bunny is still there among the
grasses and dried weeds
Still

When the rabbit died it meant new
life, could this bunny be a sign
nibbling away, hanging in there
banged up but in one piece, cute but
quietly going day to day, surviving
one day after another: because
Because? Well, because there's really
nothing else to do but that!
Taking what's there and looking
around for more, looking for where
there is more, more of what will keep
us going, Now, today, tomorrow
Really looking ahead not running
away not hiding not letting the
elements take over without a
determined stand
Like a Bunny with an attitude

Has this bunny been around? Yeah
How long will it be around? Don't
know
The bunny isn't stressing the calendar
or the cold, the cement or the traffic
the people or even me gawking at it
like it was some miraculous sign from
above
No, nothing so profound It's just
there eating out of the dirt

Here I am sitting, eating, wondering
maybe someone's watching me staring
out the window wishing summer hopes
But Winter won't see what was again
until the spring time

This bunny finds a patch of food
everyday
I search around like a blind woman in
bright sun wondering what's a human
being, what's a woman, what's a
bunny?
And it's the bunny's heart that I keep
thinking about, the bunny's heart the
unbelievable strength to endure
the courage to forage even on what's
dead and dry
The bunny's heart to live, to be, to
return to that sidewalk and take what
it has to give because today, that's all
there is to offer

To take it heartily
to live with the unknown without
excuses and assume its place in the
world
The bunny's heart, how tiny it must
fit inside its little fast racing body
Could fit 10 inside my dry skinned
empty hands

Could my one hand hold 10 bunny
hearts at once? My heart is human in
size but too flat to handle the magic
My heart human in size, larger than
chickenheart, smaller than this
bunny's, this bunnyheart's heat, this
bunnyheart's power
My heart is human and so easily
frightened by the cold wind, by the
passing days and years that have worn
me down and left me brokenhearted

My heart is human but it is not
humane
I could eat this bunny and I could rob
its fur and fashion it to keep me
warm, proud and vain and I can taunt
this bunny I can trap it, can watch it
suffer and walk right past it looking
superior but feeling relieved that it
was caught, not me
I could devour this animal head and
heart and still be hungry
Yet little bunny's heart pumps its
blood of the ages straight through the
night, alone, inside a wrecked car
squeezing in between the driver's seat
and the floor pedals, huddled inside a
nest of plastic shopping bags
newspapers, rags, waiting out the
night, tranquil, awaiting sleep, yet
ready to book, split, leap if it must to
preserve it's wild life, if a prowler
another animal, another heart hungry
be it man or beast
approaches on the prowl for the same
thing: a place to sleep tonite

Without question the bunny waits for
the morning sun to begin the search
for food and a better place to spend

the night tonite,
I wouldn't survive 10 minutes out here
alone and the bunny knows it
I hide behind my size and rumored
strength and knowledge but the bunny
knows what is real and what is hype in
the animal world

For now I can only hang out, can only
observe from the outside, must keep
my distance until I can follow its
tracks, because I have yet to
understand how hard beautiful is to
come by

And so it seems to me that this little
bunny is a very wise bunny,
A very wise living being, out here in
the world, unaided but not unable to
live
An example for living is that bunny

Karen Green is a lifelong resident of the Bronx. She graduated with a BA in Political Science from Marymount Manhattan College and has an MS in Early Childhood Education from CUNY at Lehman College. She is an advocate of environmental education, and conducted creative workshops at the New York Botanical Garden in the Family Garden for the WritersCorps.

I define myself as someone who is deeply interested in the education of our children, who believes that children can reach their full potential if given the right opportunities.

For many years I didn't have an environmental education. Then I worked as a volunteer at the Botanical Gardens and saw how that could be a kind of therapy for those who needed to reach out and grow. After returning to college, I continued my volunteer work at the Botanical Gardens and, in view of all the curriculum problems in the city, became deeply interested in writing a curriculum that would give children in K through 6 a basis for science, math, art, music, history and literature through studying plants and nature.

Several years ago I taught my curriculum to 350 children a week for the Horticultural Society in the Harlem public schools. I worked there for two years—the most exciting two years I'd had in a long time—until the Horticultural Society lost their funding. So when the opportunity of WritersCorps presented itself, it was something I wanted to do, because it seemed like a natural progression for me. The only problem was that I didn't think I belonged in this group of writers, for whom writing was their life's work.

WritersCorps has been very helpful in placing me in a site where I could utilize ideas from my curriculum. Unfortunately there wasn't enough time to put into practice many of the projects which might have been helpful to the children. For instance, I had hoped to get them to design a garden, but with only 20 minutes per session it wasn't possible.

I worked with two other teachers. Typically we'd go down to the family garden and sit under a gazebo. One of the science teachers would do an experiment with the children. The other teacher would take them to a plot of land where they'd plant radishes. That was very exciting for them, because they saw the radishes grow, and got to take them home. I would either read them a book, or some proverbs, take them to the pond, or through the meadow and ask them to smell and touch and feel what it was like to be there.

As far as being a supportive role model, and sharing the children's excitement, my experience was a plus. If the goal of WritersCorps is to have them communicate in a way that more people can understand them through the written word, however, then I wasn't very successful.

I do think that these children each have a voice. Some of them were willing to give more, to connect. I read a book called *"The First

Forest," about why certain trees remain green all year, and why some lose their leaves—it's really about selfishness for sunlight, and the damage that causes to the forest. They loved that book. If I had more time, I think they might have written a story, a response to the feelings in the book.

I relied more on art then I did on literature, because art came naturally to them, and I figured I would progress from art to literature, which did not happen. They loved the ponds, the frogs, the turtles and the lily pads. I'd say, "OK, now go back to your seats and see if you can draw a picture of what you just saw." Some of them made such detailed pictures.

What I've gotten back is the knowledge that children in nature are a natural. Basically, the children were happy in this venue. They didn't act out—they were interested. Environmental education is equally important as English and social studies and drama and history.

Children have to be taught now how to preserve the resources in our environment. They have to realize that sometimes, less is more, that things from the environment can be used over and over again if they're used properly, and that the environment is something that not only supplies us with resources, but creates a beautiful background for living. They need to feel this in their neighborhoods and their communities. They don't want to see blight—blight is depressing.

I'm not saying environmental education is the most important, but it's worthy of being part of a child's education. If environmental education is going to continue, I think the private sector has to be involved, because it's taking a very long time to change curriculum, and break down bureaucracy in the schools.

The environment inside the classroom is equally as important as the environment outside. I don't think there are enough things that give spirit to the children in their classrooms. Building a mini farm, or planting an herb garden or bulbs, or making potpourri, or an anatomically correct flower, or a picture of a rain forest—all this adds to the beauty of their immediate environment. It helps them see that they can create their future, if they want.

Karen Green

Thoughts from the New York Botanical Garden

(A picture of a bouquet of flowers)
I want to give this to my mom for she could feel and smell them and fall in love with them.

by Jessica

I'm going to draw a little forest with little creatures and birds where people come and see what the nice forest without polluting and there will be no cutting down trees that will be the future forest.

by Aleya

I want to give someone these flowers. Who is it? What I was drawing is flowers that I saw all around. They are all hard to draw so I tried my best. They're for my mother.

by Andrew

Rain in spring is as precious as oil (Proverb)

—because it lets flowers and trees grow
—spring it lets sun make light for trees and flowers to grow
—oil is good for heat and to cook for.

(unsigned)

Encouraging Nurturing Behavior of Two-to Seven-Year-Olds by Introducing Plants and Flowers
(Excerpts)

by Karen Green

SUMMARY. The purpose of this project was to design a curriculum which encourages nurturing behavior of two- to seven-year-olds by introducing plants and flowers and to design an observation instrument to be used by the teachers involved in the implementation of the curriculum.

A six-week curriculum comprising thirty lessons was designed to use materials to aid children in the development of nine nurturing behaviors. Each week's lessons included sensory activities that were meant to foster practical life experiences. Books, music, outdoor activities, cooking and fantasy play were incorporated into the curriculum for at least one hour each day. The children were encouraged to learn positive social skills.

Every day we are told from one source or another that many of our children are living in home and school situations which are unacceptable—that they are succumbing to societal pressures, including drugs and other forms of violence, and are not achieving their unique potential. These feelings of helplessness and frustration experienced by us, as educators and parents, result from our perceived inability to battle these mounting societal pressures.

There is no one answer that will resolve the situation. All we can do—and what we must do—is take steps and make changes, both in and outside the classroom, that positively effect the development of our youth. I have prepared a "plant play" curriculum entitled "Tools to Grow, Curriculum for Early Childhood," that I feel will help to develop nurturing behavior and social skills and give children the feeling of empowerment that they need to thrive in our rapidly changing society.

★

Children can learn the elements of practical life through a curriculum of plant/play, as well as developing an appreciation of the beauty, wonder and perpetuation of life. Being surrounded by plants and flowers on a daily basis, children see the care that goes into keeping them healthy and strong—much like his/her caregivers.

It is important that early on, a child is aware of what makes them feel good and bad, stressed or unstressed, frustrated or not. Through observation of the child, a teacher can help the child to verbalize his or her needs and learn about how he or she works. Naming things, developing sensory awareness through observing, listening and feeling through smelling and tasting materials that are living and natural broadens their range in language development. The child is then able to communicate with others and begin to develop long and lasting caring and sharing relationships.

In an urban environment, particularly in high density inner city school districts, if we want ultimately for children to care for each other and their environment, they must be nurtured by the beauties of those elements as well. If we can help them to create an environment that can nourish and provide beauty, we are giving them tools to keep their spirits high.

Majora J. Carter, a graduate of Wesleyan University, is currently working toward her MA in Creative Writing at NYU and writing her first novel. As a member of WritersCorps she is the Writer-in-Residence at the Phipps Community Development Corporation's West Farm Beacon Program, teaching classes in Screenwriting, Poetry and Fiction and supervising Beacon's first video production, "*The Kidnapper.*"

Photo by Wayne Providence

I'm a writer because there's not much else I enjoy doing. Film-making is another one of my loves, but when I think about making films, I think of directing films I've written myself, so writing is the basis of it all.

My experience with WritersCorps has reminded me how hard it can be for kids growing up now. I'm working with kids whose first impulse is definitely not to write, but to talk. They haven't been taught that writing is a means of expression, a way to make things more permanent. A lot of them live so in-the-moment that they tend to forget things can last. It's not simply forgetting what you did 5 minutes ago, but that the past no longer serves a purpose.

Because so many of my kids didn't want to write, I brought in a tape recorder and had them tell their stories and poems. Each time I'd transcribe the tapes, they would look at the written work as though they'd never seen it before! After shock, came recognition, then a sense of satisfaction. By the end of class their papers would be crumpled from running around showing each other—"I did this!" It was wild. It reminded me of my own childhood, when I'd run to show my mother the second I wrote something, how much joy that gave me—to know this was something that I'd done without help from anybody on the planet, and I owned it! I like giving that to these kids. I know that some will continue to write long after I'm gone. I'm excited because a lot of them think much more creatively than before. Now they'll say, "I was thinking of writing a story like this. . ."

The kids have taught me so much—especially patience. I couldn't believe they weren't listening to me. Nothing seemed to work, and I would leave crying a lot. I'd think, "They're not going know that they have a voice, that people should be listening to them—and it's all my fault!"

It took me weeks and weeks before I got them to write, or to the point where they were actually thinking creatively. I realized later, they were getting to know me, feeling me out. They had to learn that I wasn't there to judge them, or grade them or make them feel bad because they couldn't do certain things. My expectations had to change. I didn't have this kind of teaching experience and it took a lot of perseverance on all levels—personal, spiritual, educational.

I had to find out what they wanted to do and work around that. When I discovered that, it was great. They enjoyed it, I enjoyed it. I probably should have done that from the beginning but I didn't think you could do that with students. You learn.

I think the mission of WritersCorps is to encourage writing as an important means of creative expression. It's an art, but at the same time it's also about personal growth or recovery, and there are ways to combine all those things for people who aren't planning to be professional writers. Just writing in a diary or journal gives you something to look back on. You can't help but learn from that.

Writing is a way to remember. Every now and then I look back at things I've written years ago and see where I was. I find that exciting—to know there's a path that everyone's going to take and how you can see that in a person's writing. Public policy, journal writing, or even advertising—written words give you a flavor for what's going on at any point in time; whether it's personal or on a broader scale, it's history. I don't like the idea of anyone's history being lost. Oral traditions are amazing, but I don't see any harm in writing down an oral tradition as it was meant to be told.

I've recently been working on an oral history project with other WritersCorps members which we're shaping into a play, and in which my dad is a participant. My dad's 88 and I'm discovering all these great things that would have died with him were it not for this project. It's not going to create world peace, but it's important because that's how people live—and live on.

Metamorphosis

1.

by Paula

If I were a
caterpillar I would
turn into a
teenager because
I would get to go
out with my
friends and I
could go to the
store by myself.

2.

by Jereyle

If I were a giraffe
I would turn into
a cheetah because
they run so fast
and they could
beat an elephant
with a long trunk.

3.

by Sahara

If I were a
caterpillar I would
turn into a
butterfly because
I would love to
fly.

4.

by George

If I were a
caterpillar I would
turn into a lion
because lions like
to eat people and
I like to eat. Food
is people too.

Tea and Poetry Reading

Exciting
Shakiara A.

Blueberry
Blackberry
Cherry-Berry-Mooseberry

Play Around
Shakiara A.

On the playground
I see things in the yard
On the playground
I see beautiful trees
I see flowers
On my playground
I see birds and eagles
On my playground
I see things in the playground
I see beautiful flowers in the yard
I also see birds flying in the yard

Untitled
by Natasha R.

Oh dear, oh dear!
Please don't fight here!
Oh dear, oh dear!
Let's go to the rainbow over there!
Oh dear, oh dear!

Sad
by Aliyah F.

Boohoo, boohoo!
I am very sad
Very, very sad
And I don't know why I am crying.
Boohoo, boohoo!
Now I remember!
A little boy was teasing me
And I don't know why
Boohoo, boohoo!
Now I remember!
I was teasing him first
Now I know why I am crying!
Boohoo, boohoo!

Under the Rug
by Emilia C.

There was a man who had a rug that had something under it that would rise. This kept on happening for a while and then it stopped. Two weeks passed and it happened again. Every time the rug would rise, it would hit the chair that he was sitting on. The man got so mad and tired of it that he picked up the chair he was sitting on and was about to hit the bump on the rug. But before he hit it, he thought to himself that he should check and see what it was first. As he was about to look, he jumped back because the little thing started to move. He lifted the rug anyway and saw that it was a snake that had been trapped in the rug. The man was scared, but so was the snake. It attacked him and choked him, leaving him without breath. The snake had choked him so tightly with it's tail that it left him on the rug in his house, breathless and without color. The man was dead and the snake stayed in the house and waited for the next person or family to move in. He knew that they would get angry at the bump on the rug and try to attack it. The snake really had a plan for the next person or family. . .

516 Casanova Street
A Novel in Progress
(Excerpt from Chapter 1)
by Majora J. Carter

The turquoise ribbon of daylight slid up through the sky. Theresa watched it glide by as she stood on the back porch. She fidgeted with the safety pin that held the collar of her housecoat together and shifted her arms so that her elbows wouldn't stick out of the threadbare holes in the sleeves. She lit a cigarette from the supply that her youngest daughter, Cathy, thought she had hidden in her room. It was stale, they always were. Theresa was certain that Cathy smoked only to make herself look tough and probably smoked so little that she didn't notice that her cigarettes were steadily disappearing.

She had taken the cigarette when she went to check in on Cathy late last night. Cathy was not in her room. *That girl sure has a nice way of being on punishment,* Theresa had thought.

She took one last deep drag: the smoke mixed with the cold air already in her lungs. It invigorated her. She shouldn't smoke, her angina wasn't getting any better. She was relieved that Rebecca hadn't arrived from school yet. Since Theresa's heart attack, Rebecca acted more like a mother rather than a daughter or a friend. Theresa didn't feel like being hassled—not even by her favorite child.

She dropped the cigarette butt behind the barbecue pit that stood in the far corner of the yard. It joined many others just like it. Theresa made a mental note to remove them all long before barbecue season began.

If somebody told me twenty or thirty years ago that I would be spending this Thanksgiving day where I am right now, sneaking cigarettes from my daughter, cooking my behind off for a bunch of ingrates, I would have told that somebody to go screw a flea. Really, I would've. Look at me, old, fat and ugly. Hard to believe I wasn't always like this. Nope, not always.

She hoped the smoke didn't cling to her.

So what if it does.

She walked back inside the house.

★

Theresa sat at the table opening up cans of peaches and emptying them into a bowl. She leaned back in her chair so she could rest

her head on the wall behind her. A moment to relax turned into a
vacation as she closed her eyes and remembered that she had made
a dress the exact same color as those peaches almost thirty years ago.

"Isn't anything *cooked* yet?"

Theresa looked up to see Cathy, dressed in a nightgown, rum-
maging through the refrigerator. She had waltzed into the kitchen,
pretending to wipe sleep from her eyes, yawning and stretching with
gusto.

Theresa, annoyed that Cathy had both interrupted her daydream
and had the audacity to act as though she had done nothing wrong,
looked for something to throw at her. She settled on a roll of paper
towels. It missed Cathy and hit the refrigerator door.

"Why you always got to be throwing things?" Cathy picked up
the paper towels and put them back on the table. "You never hit
nothing." Cathy made an elaborate show of rolling her eyes.

Cathy didn't realize how close Theresa was to slapping them out
of their sockets.

Cathy's truancy caused her to fail all of her classes last quarter.
Theresa put Cathy on punishment because whipping didn't seem to
work on her at all anymore. Theresa planned for the next time.
Maybe she would whip her first and then force her to sleep on a cot
in the bedroom along with Theresa and her husband, Thomas. And
then maybe she would walk her to school and attend all of her
classes with her. Theresa laughed at her own plan: she knew Cathy
would die of embarrassment before any real changes in her behavior
could be made.

"Did you have fun last night, Catherine?"

Theresa watched Cathy's exploration through the refrigerator
come to a standstill, but in a moment she was back to normal. She
could only guess the expression on her face. Cathy remained bent
down, peering into the refrigerator.

"What are you talking about?"

"Did you have fun spending your punishment out hanging with
your hoodlum friends?"

"I was *out hanging* in my room."

"Don't mock me."

"Don't give me nothing to mock."

Watch yourself Theresa.

"Did you have a good time last night?"

"Yeah, I slept like a baby. Thanks for asking. I didn't know you
cared."

216

"Don't play me for a fool, little girl."

"You do all right all by yourself."

Theresa's hand involuntarily tightened around the can that she was about to open.

"You live in my house. You abide by my rules. You need to learn some respect, Catherine."

Cathy stood up straight, closing the refrigerator door. She was already six inches taller than her mother. She stood up to her full height, tilting her head up and back. She narrowed her eyes and spoke:

"Why don't you just get off my back."

Max was at the door, letting herself in, along with a strong wind that carried dead leaves. Carrying grocery bags filled with food she had already prepared, she struggled to close the door behind her. The second oldest daughter in the Patterson household happily hummed the refrain from Vickie Sue Robinson's "Turn the Beat Around," as she strolled toward the kitchen. She made it to the door just in time to see Theresa throw the can. She had aimed for Cathy's head. Theresa flailed the air, trying to grab it back.

Cathy ducked, just as the can hit the refrigerator behind her. It bounced off the refrigerator and hit her spine. Cathy let out a small cry and Theresa shuddered at the impact.

"Oh my God. . . " Theresa stumbled around the table to reach her.

Cathy sidled away from her on her hands and knees, not taking her eyes away from Theresa for a second. She crawled to the kitchen door and pulled herself up to her feet. Cathy pointedly refused Max's help, but she was willing to use her as a barrier between herself and her mother. She glanced past Theresa to the dent on the refrigerator and then back at Theresa. She stared at her for a long second and made no effort to hide her contempt.

"It didn't even hurt," Cathy said to Theresa, then hissed in Max's ear, "Your mother's crazy."

Theresa pressed her lips together as she watched Cathy move out of her view. She wanted to say something, but was afraid she would only make things worse.

I could've killed her.

Theresa clapped her hands over her mouth.

Max stood in the doorway and tried to shake off the shock. She prayed for patience before she walked into the kitchen. Theresa turned to the refrigerator and traced her finger along the dent.

Max glanced at the dent and then at Theresa.

"What's wrong with you?" Max yelled at Theresa's back. "You could have killed her!"

Theresa opened the refrigerator and pulled two sticks of butter out of the container.

"Leave me alone, Max," she said. "Just leave me alone."

"No, I will not leave you alone. You just can't go around throwing heavy objects at people's heads."

"I didn't hit her."

"Only by the grace of God. What is wrong with you, Mommy? You're losing it. Every time I turn around, you're trying to beat up on Cathy or one of the kids. You're supposed to be the adult."

"I *am* an adult, I just let your sister get to me too much."

"So you threw a can at her head?"

"I missed, didn't I?"

"Mommy, why—"

"What'd you do to your hair?"

"What?"

"You did something to your hair."

"Yeah, highlights. We can talk about them later. What about—"

"I like it. Now, what did I ask you to bring again?"

Theresa had effectively ended the conversation. In the past, Max would have tried to make Theresa see that there was still work to be done. Now, she knew that there would be no reason to try to belabor the point. Theresa would not budge. Max conceded the battle with a sigh.

"I brought the ham, the hop'n'johns, candied yams and two sour cream pies."

"Oh, you'll make Rebecca's day, she's been asking me to make a sour cream pie since Easter. Yours will do. They're almost as good as mine."

Max reached around her mother's back and grabbed hold of Theresa's braid. It hung down to the small of her back. It was gray all the way to the ends.

"So when are you going to let me do your hair?"

"When I lose about thirty years."

"Oh please, honey, you got platinum blond written all over you *right now.*"

"Don't make me laugh."

218

They laughed. Theresa laughed loudest.

Max remembered the only photograph of her mother in her youth that she had ever seen. She had herself draped over the hood of a baby blue Bel Air, and she was wearing an orange halter-top dress. She smiled as though she held a juicy secret from whomever gazed upon her picture. And she looked at the viewer through her left eye only; the right side of her face was covered by a tremendous wave of black hair that hung way past her breast. To Max, she looked like she had just stepped out of a Prince video. Theresa had told her that her boyfriend, the owner of the car, teased her that he bought that particular car because he thought she'd look good in it. Theresa had told him that it didn't matter what he drove because she could make a wreck look good just by walking near it.

Max sometimes saw glimpses of the young woman in the picture, in the face of the woman in the kitchen. She was still there, somewhere. Still beautiful. Still happy. Still strong. Whenever she emerged, Max would inwardly rejoice and outwardly attempt to hold her captive, keep her interested, amused. It never worked for long. Her mother would crawl back into her hiding place just as smoothly as she slid out of it.

She looked at her mother in her ratty housecoat in her drafty old house, which sat in a neighborhood whose heyday had vanished years ago. Walking around a kitchen frequented almost exclusively by a family full of users, some with dreams too big for them, others too big for their dreams. After seeing the picture for the first time, Max wanted to ask her, "What were you thinking then? What were your plans? What were your dreams? Did you ever have any dreams? You must have wanted something for yourself." She had yet to find the courage to ask those questions.

Mary Yorizzo Hebert was born in Bronxville, New York, attended CUNY, Lehman College and is a graduate of SUNY, Albany. She is the author of *"Horatio Rides the Wind,"* published by Templar PLC, and a contributor to the Pocket Books' anthology, *"I've Always Meant to Tell You, Letters to Our Mothers,"* due out May 1997. For the WritersCorps she conducted writing workshops at MindBuilders Creative Arts Center in the Northeast Bronx.

Photo by Wayne Providence

I'm a writer because the world I was born into wasn't enough. My father was a carpenter, my mother a housewife, and it was basically working class life—there weren't many literary influences—so I felt I had to create a world. It gave me a lot of comfort, and still does. As a writer you get to be many different things—an archeologist, a scientist. It's a constant hunger to explore.

Writers seek truths, and by that I mean we match up what we see with what we feel, or what society says is reality with what we perceive to be; we try to figure out why people do what they do, what makes people survive odds. For example, I wrote a short prose poem inspired by the kids I'm working with. One day one of the kids was acting up. As I walked toward him, he backed up and said, "Are you gonna hit me now?" Immediately I wondered, what was the truth of this young man's life? In the poem, I use the image of a train running off a platform. The line that expresses the truth the best goes, "We're not the passengers, we're the train." To me that means these children are at a point in their lives when they could be misdirected, go off track; they're making choices that could affect their whole lives. We should pay attention to that.

We'd be in a lot worse shape were it not for writers. Writers are scary, always uncovering things. When you spend a good deal of your time in contemplation, you become a receiver. I'm a strong believer in the collective unconscious, as Jung passed it on to us. When you connect, and words just flow out, you say something that has resonance to a bigger audience.

Writers are a very powerful force, which is why there's often a backlash culturally, and why there's all this going on in Washington now—that the arts are expendable, that our society can live without it, or without government subsidizing it. It's because writers and artists get to issues, and if enough of them are supported and working, then their audiences will also be developing. The forces that work against fear and separatism are the creative forces. Writing as a creative act is making something from nothing, and if a child can learn to write a story, she can learn to create her life.

When I learned about WritersCorps, I thought, "Someone in Washington really gets it." The idea is really revolutionary. To get a group of 18 writers to agree on anything is quite a feat, and to get them working inside a bureaucracy is even more startling. In a funny way—at least in the Bronx—I think it's working. Each one of us could probably see, just as we're closing our projects, what effect we've had. It would be a shame to stop here, to have opened up all those doors inside people, then suddenly say, "Sorry, we're out of money, we're not going to do this any more."

I joined WritersCorps because the idea of teaching outside the bureaucracy of schools was appealing—without the curriculum and all that crap. To take all I had learned, as far as the creative process goes, and share that, was an exciting idea. It was also great to have an opportunity to work with kids, because I write children's books. I felt immediately it was going to stretch me, to pass on what I do, and make it fun.

I feel I've had a pretty tangible impact on the kids. In the beginning they'd look at me screwy when I'd say, "We're going to do this. I want you to write this. . . " Toward the end they'd ask, "Are we gonna write today?" The whole process is mind-boggling, but it does happen.

So from my personal experience, I think the program's been a success, but I wouldn't want to stop there. I don't think the Bronx, San Francisco and Washington, DC, are the only places in the country that need this. The suburbs could use this. Where I grew up, it's a cultural black hole: there's high school and bars, and nothing in-between. They should look at these individual successes and take risks. It would be nice to see the government take risks with something other than war zones, to build people's self-worth. We've all taken risks, and a lot of us have had success. That's the only way to move forward.

If I Could Fly
by Chris H.

If I could fly
I would fly in peace
and quiet in the sky.
I would be a bird,
a blue bird.

If I Could Fly
by Melissa P.

If I could fly
I would be
happy and
happy for
ever. I would see
birds
clouds
and that
is what
I think.

Mirror, Mirror
by Jamal D.

Mirror Mirror Mirror
in the wall
What is in the new new wall?
What is in this mirror?
Please come out. Whoever you are.
I hope that you are a tiger and a lion too. Please be it.

Rosa Parks
by Simone D.

There once was a lady named Rosa Parks. She was a very famous
woman and one day she was coming home from work and this white man
came on the bus. The driver said, can you get up and give this white man a
seat? She said no, and they put her in jail.

Harriet Tubman
by Jason L.

What I like about Harriet Tubman.
She helped free black slaves and she
died in 1913. I love my father.
I love my Dad and friends.

Dream
by Sean M.

Once I had a dream about Playland when a man shot a girl. She was seven. She was good in the neighborhood. The spirit of the girl came to haunt him. He got shot by the girl. The same way. The end.

Dream Catcher
by Diakka A.

Once I had a dream that I'm on top of a mountain. I had just hiked up it and was very tired when I saw the American bird the eagle and tripped. I fell all the way down the mountain and died, then I woke up. I wish the dream catcher would get that dream.

The Mystery of Paris
by Anthony V.

This story is about a man that goes into the woods. He can't go home because of the weather. So he ends up sleeping there. As soon as he woke up he saw a rattlesnake right in front of him. He ran and ran until he tripped over a rock. The snake bit him on his leg. Luckily he had a phone that didn't need a cord and he called the Ambulance.

They hurried over. The Ambulance took him to the hospital. People tracked down the snake and killed it. As soon as the man got out of the hospital he saw his wife, and they kissed. They lived happily ever after. The End.

Poem
by Celene R.

The sky is blue
the cow just mooed
It just turned noon 5 minutes ago
after a while you soon
be booed by a scary old
ghost you see in the
sky. It's just a picture you
see in the sky, but if
you really look at it
it's really your imagination. . .

Poem
by Alexis A.

The sky is Blue
it is so new
so glow in the night.

The Earth
by Aritha A.

The Earth is wonderful.
We are wonderful
So keep the earth clean
Because the earth is in our hand.

Saying Stones
by Jamal D.

I am a stone and my name is Mike and
it is a boy. I come from Jamaica. It is
so nice to hold a stone, you could feel Very Very Happy.
I like when people Hold me, it is the nicest life.
The End.

226

Dream: Children's Rites
by Mary Hebert

I wake with a picture of an elevated platform
the edges torn like a huge piece of paper with the
thought sharp as February:
children write on an open book
that is an elevated subway platform
a train careening off the edges.
Children write reaching for colored pens
hungry as bees seeking the promise of bright flowers
their fingers restless
children write in-between fidgets and act-outs,
questions which are all the same question,
am I good enough
am I good enough
do you love me enough
is this stupid enough this is stupid
am I stupid to say this want
love so children write on the edge of their seats
in the cafeteria platform with a train careening
off the edges children write
do you see me do you see
we are not passengers, we are the train?

Do you if I run shout out of turn
throw pens under the table do you see
my colors children write the sun
the words nice and happy curtains
to their heart a longing do you see me
do you love me are you going to hit me now?
Children write:
see me, please,
see me now.

Facing the Crocodile Man

by Mary Hebert

In my marrow
what sings?

1. The Dance

My soul knows Egypt
though I've never been, why
I feel at home in museums always
gravitate to the mummy section, fingers
reaching for the fat secrets
 of hieroglyphics

I first meet the crocodile man
one day while passing through the book of
the dead. In order to live forever
according to the ancient Egyptians, your
heart must be lighter than the feather of
truth; if not, it's the job of the crocodile
man to eat it.

He sits confidently at the end of the
god line watching the scales
tip, knowing it won't be long before
the next juicy heart comes his way fat
with lies.

I think I danced with him once, the reptile
face that eats cheating hearts. I do
fancy steps and dips, hoping he won't
look at the inner tube of lies around
my heart that's kept me
above water

It's time to sink his eyes
say, showing his best crocodile teeth.
That's when I run for it, promising
myself the next time we meet I will

have cleaned up my act, taken swimming
lessons at least.

2. The Ride

Back in the safety of my apartment my cat
sends me messages in pictures; the crocodile
man doesn't phase her with her quarter-sized
heart. The way she perches on the arm of my green
chair calls me back in time to some ancestral
tomb where we were buried. I want
to sit and dream this, but it's time
instead for my climb uptown on
the number 2.

Being underground alive
makes my heart feel heavy with
life. I scan the amazing caravan
of faces and imagine under our forest-
colored coats, behind our sleepy eyes we are
all in the same dream and before I
know it the car is full of light.

Being the height of tree tops gives me a
thrill despite the rattle screech
so familiar it's made its own private groove
in my memory. The signs say **Jackson
Prospect** but the line of seats in the line
of cars reminds me of the line to
the crocodile man. I picture him sitting
at the end of White Plains Road jaw
open, ready to swallow us no
questions asked, assuming anyone riding
this train is going
nowhere.

I want to wake everyone up, tell them
how it's time to show this crocodile
man a thing or two, how everyone in this car is
going somewhere, how quickly we can lighten

our hearts, how deep in their red folds they
can cut through old ideas of black
and white like a steel train wheel cuts through
time matter-of-factly, in love with the electricity
that powers its movement.

3. The Dream

If we peel back our skin, crack
the cage of spoken language what is
left but something more
sacred and ancient, a language as
light as the feather of truth

if we peel back our skin what
color are bones, what color
marrow, what dialect does our blood
speak as it runs the miracle of
codes and cells through us

what color the heart?
the crocodile man
doesn't care what color
mask we wear, all he
wants
wants
wants,
is the
truth.

Rain

by Mary Hebert

the rain is all that needs to be said
the night my father
asked me, *who are you?*

slants of water against the wind
the stark movement of steel
on an iron rail

I, the water returning home
he, the rail, cold and disappearing
into the horizon

after the hours I spend
holding his hand,
smoothing his white tendrils
he, slipping
into the corridor
of fear

where a nurse
watches, amused
that he calls for his mother,
indifferent to the daughter's panic
at seeing a father so fallen
to this
a man become this
a bibbed child barelegged and screaming
against the cold green tiles

I search wildly
through the forest
of stories he has told
for a picture of what his wild dark eyes see

knowing it is the untold dark
he faces, the tunnels of a mind

gouged by the twin
hooves of booze and chemicals
as his body shrivels
beneath the stones of his
survival

still my fingers try
pressing the knowledge of my skin
into the cold sweat of his
umbrian forehead
who are you?

the question falls, a buzzard
after a raw heart

still
the rain,
the rain,
is all

soft and permanent
on the grey cement
that rises around me
making a city
of my thoughts,
a flocking of bird memories
hungry for spring,

still
I listen for the far away parting
of rusted lips
the calling
that is, finally

my name.

Wayne **Providence** is the son of an only son, and the father of an only son. An educator, writer/poet, photographer and a Bronx-ite from New York City, he received a BFA from the School of Visual Arts and an MFA from Hunter College. He is a product of the Sonia Sanchez and Quincy Troupe Writers Workshop. As a WritersCorps member, he created a Pen Pal Project at the New York City Housing Authority.

To the Roman Empire 10/5/96

glad to share the Magikk

from Divine Providence

Photo by Jules Allen

233

I love writing. One thing, I love to paint with words. I'm always searching for a fresher type of language, conjuring up images that are different from what we've seen, with words we already know. I write because the art form of writing still needs to be explored, and now I know what I'm doing with it. I didn't consciously plan to be a writer, it just formed on its own. In writing, I move from one page to longer works that deal with performance, using dance, painting, music and the written word.

Society needs writers to document and explore the creative realm—writers are like painters. Artists show society what it needs to see and helps put people in tune with themselves. What you think, somebody else may have thought. Without art there is no culture.

I don't know why I chose to join WritersCorps. I feel it was fate—it was my time. The Corps is very good; as a vehicle, it lets me do what I like to do within the community, creating a place where young people can create. Kids don't write, everything is fed to them. Through WritersCorps I give back, to show that these kids all have something to offer themselves and their community. This is a way for them to experience their feelings of self worth.

Hopefully in our time with WritersCorps, we can bring about changes in some things. The choices of sites vary, which brings a mix to ink on paper, from the youth to their ancestors.

WritersCorps can open up doors and stimulate minds, offer a quick glimpse that can change someone's outlook. The situation in the Bronx is difficult because we are dealing with all types of shit that the kids deal with in the neighborhoods they grow and live in everyday. The Pen Pals Project is so gratifying because the kids are waiting to hear from people with whom they've just made friends. They're getting to know their neighbors in other cities, states and countries.

Pen Pal Poems
by Tiffany S.

I am a high top sneaker people can wear
with different clothing. I come in different colors.
I come in two tone colors. I am a reebok.
My color is purple and white.
I am a low top sneaker people can wear.
I come in different colors I come in all colors.
Like black, green, yellow, white, pink, blue, red
black and red stripe colors. I can be worn in
hot or cold weather I come in hightop and
low top.

A Poem
by Jessica S.

In a dark, dark house. There
was a dark, dark, room. And in
that dark, dark room, there was
a dark, dark, box. And in that
dark, dark, box There was—
     a
     GHOST!

About My Hands
by Jakayrah C.

My hands have lines and I could
pick things. And my hands could smack
people and hit them. I got knuckles
and I have a pinkie and a thumb.

     this is My hand.
     and my rings.

Love. . . Poems
by Jennifer M.

Love

Love is everywhere. In the clouds, wind,
houses, marriages, relationships, families, and many
more places. There are always two people to
make love-relationships. They also in friends.
There is another love like I Love food,
sleep, and play. I Love food because it stops
your hunger and they taste very good.
I Love to sleep because on school mornings,
I can't sleep. I love to play because I
need exercise.

I hate. . .

I hate school because it is confusing. I hate
school lunch because it taste nasty. I hate
drug dealers because they sell drugs. I hate the lunch
lady because she screams at people for no
reason.

The Beauty in Me. . .

I am a very pretty girl. My
family thinks I am beautiful too. A
boy in my class thinks I am very
beautiful too.

Poem
by Jacqual C.

My hand can punch
I love my hand
My hand can fight
My hand can touch
My hand can smack
My hand can beat

Dear Pen Pal,

I am one of the new Pen Pal at Betances 146.

Looking for a Pen Pal From Beach 41st.

My name is Muriel, I am eight years old.

I go to PS27 and I Live in the Bronx.

I Like to play in the Park with my friend
and I Love to eat ice cream and cake. And my
Birthday is on March 23, and my mom Like the
color Black White and Blue. And I Like the color
Red pink and orange and what is your name?
and what grade you are in? How old are you?
now it is time for me to say thank you for being
my Pen Pal. I will Like to write you a letter. And
My mother take care of me. And I got a sister name
Shari and I got a Bother and his name is Eddie and
I got a Bother name Edwin + I got a Grandma + I got a
Grandpa and I got a uncle name Smokey.

Love, Muriel

Poems by Wayne Providence

on side one the dream   reach for it
we met 'round mid-nite on red river-road
and play giantsteps to each other
our first born was a doubledear boy   we listened

what's more precious
than whispers
of things not said
and to bathe one's feelings
in the steam of passion

you've become
this attraction
vogue
flirtatious images

i touch you
you jump
i blow breezes in your ear
then watch crazy-ness take over

your lips soft
your tongue dances with mine
we tag all over each other

a squeeze
becomes a grip
a hold on tight
a tight hold in cradle moments
i can go on
and on   and on
and on   and on

barefoot we walk black-sand
and invite curiosity to a place
of unprepared essence
that supplies life

we make moves
create distance
that have no boundaries
while undertones shoot for something whole

along narrow escapes of differences
broken noises creep
air becomes non-descript
upon entrances to games
where no rules exist

all ventures are crossings
that leap
then disappear underfoot

we are half-bodies
searching outcomes
leaning against delicate moments
stored for desperate occasions

many covers unfold
beneath a sunday's heat sound carves a way
for stair-step music
riverting mixtures
cutting speed
finding a way into cut-time

i saw Bigg n' PretTY
sweat greased her face
conversation floated
lookee   lookee   lookee
what do you see
when she appeared
she waved to everyone

as dawn breaks & the sun peeks a new-day   undertones of free
expressions waltz that thin line that parts light & dark/

brown bombers wearing forest-green jumpsuits in fade haircuts
appear on the crest of sugarhill   leaning in a south-east breeze/
the scent of crisp fried chicken & waffles coupled with the weight
of strong black coffee beckons a rush up nostrils/ the horizon is
a old folk-tale that needs fresh definition/

beams of light begin to singe the fog's edge as it silently rolls
back transforming into a blanket of morning dew/ a looooooong
saxophone wail births full body echoes   filling unoccupied spaces
eroding the funk housed deep in the belly of the ever so vibrant
valley/

sugarhill is a place of great rendezvous   calling only those who
have power in the blood   a mother's kiss   dried fruit & a sense
of self stashed in hip pockets/ there will be no marches instead
eagle dives of silent pictures with haunting secrets/
mush-mouths with sealed lips will be recruited   we hear they
token this request warmly & in appreciation they will accept aloe
leaves as a vision/

the celebration dance will be choreographed in a style & freedom
all of its own by the illustrious Miss Harlem/   she cooooches
in a back peddle glide/ madness slips down the corners of her
mouth hardening then crystallizes   rimming her lips/ i wonder
who loved her last in a way that impressed the need to search
other avenues   & build a dance floor housed between Buy-Rite &
Ma-Bell/   she shakes   shimmies   spins across concrete to a
Mississippi sourmashguttbuckethonkeytonkblues with a heavy
bottom/

if it wasn't for time

i hung with crows friday
studied their feathers and how they lay
gave them more credit than they deserved
and presumed their blackness manifested
but they coughed up powdered dreams filled with emptiness
as void conversation hopped from shot glass rims

Wayne Providence

my window was cracked just enough
for a whisper to slip thru
then this breeze rushed up my leg
with such quickness
                    then it was gone

*"**not black and white**"* is published in a first edition of 2000 copies.